Bruce Jenkins

North Shore Chronicles
Big-Wave Surfing in HAWAII
REVISED EDITION

Frog, Ltd., Berkeley, California

North Shore Chronicles: Big-Wave Surfing in Hawaii

Published by Frog, Ltd.

Frog, Ltd. books are distributed by
North Atlantic Books
P.O. Box 12327
Berkeley, California 94712

Cover: Ken Bradshaw, Outside Log Cabins
Cover art by Hank Fotos
To order a poster of the cover photo call 800-793-7989

Cover design by Catherine Campaigne
Book design by Paula Morrison

Printed in the United States of America

Library of Congress Cataloging-in-Publication Data
Jenkins, Bruce, 1948–
    North Shore Chronicles : big-wave surfing in Hawaii / Bruce Jenkins. —
2nd ed.
        p.   cm.
    Summary: Provides updated profiles of surfers the author has met during
his many years of surfing on Oahu's North Shore.
    ISBN 1-883319-90-0 (alk. paper)
    1. Surfing—Hawaii—Juvenile literature. 2. Surfers—Hawaii—
Interviews—Juvenile literature. [1. Surfing—Hawaii.]   I. Title.
GV840.S8J46 1999
797.3'2'09969—dc21   90-53530
                                                                             CIP
                                                                             AC

Contents

Introduction 7

The Wave 11

Ken Bradshaw 19

Trevor Sifton 41

Off the Wall 51

Mark Foo 55

Tom Nellis 65

Mark Cunningham 77

Mike Stewart 93

Little Bits of History 107

Stepping Out 121

The Seasoned View 129

The *Hokule'a* 137

Darrick Doerner 143

The Eddie 159

Big Wednesday 177

The Last Wave 191

Introduction

The sport of surfing has changed signficantly since the original release of this book, but in a sense, it hasn't changed at all. I realized that on the morning of January 28, 1998, when Ken Bradshaw made big-wave history.

He was 45, a full 10 years older than when I first interviewed him. At a time when most athletes have long since retired, he was at the peak of his powers. As I reflected upon the other great surfers detailed in these pages, I saw the same timeless qualities. Mark Foo has passed on, a casualty of Maverick's, the feared big-wave spot in Northern California, in 1994. But the others have persevered, only improving in status and performance. That's what brings me back to the waves, and the people who ride them, year after year. Surfing is for life.

Ke Iki Road, not far from Waimea Bay on the North Shore of Oahu, is my personal surfing landmark. I was sleeping in a small cottage there in 1986 when a midnight "rogue" wave destroyed it, beyond repair, with me inside. I was strictly a mainstream sportswriter then, deeply connected with Hawaiian surfing but awestruck by its legends. But my experience that night gave me something to share. If anything, it heightened my fascination with big waves, and it led to a series of interviews with the North Shore's most committed surfers — not the touring professionals or visiting superstars, but an elite group within that realm, the ones who live in Hawaii and base their entire existence around riding mountainous, terrifying surf.

I'll never forget meeting Bradshaw in '88. His commanding presence and articulate nature were riveting to behold. As a brash, sometimes temperamental figure, he was not universally popular. A lot of North Shore surfers resented him, even placed him in the old-hat, over-the-hill category. How wrong they were. That raging fire still burns within Bradshaw, and he proved it that morning in '98, when he captured the largest wave ever ridden on Oahu.

Yes, quite a bit had changed. Ten years before, big-wave surfing was all about Waimea Bay and conventional equipment. Now Bradshaw had joined the tow-in movement, where surfers are strapped onto their boards (much like windsurfers) and thrown into open-ocean swells like a slingshot, water-ski style, from an accompaying power boat. The idea is to match a giant wave's speed, to execute a takeoff that would not be possible under a surfer's own power. In 1995, Bradshaw was a wide-eyed novice as he joined Darrick Doerner and Laird Hamilton on an unforgettable tow-in session at 25-foot Outside Backyards. Now he was primed and ready. With the expert help of his longtime partner, Dan Moore, Bradshaw hopped aboard a 40-foot wave at Outside Log Cabins, rode it beautifully, and set new standards on the fabled North Shore coastline.

As always, Ke Iki was my measuring stick. In 1969, the year of the largest swell of modern history, houses were literally moved across the highway. In 1986, I became an official spokesman for Ke Iki chaos. And now there was Big Wednesday '98. When I heard there had been extensive damage on Ke Iki early that morning, I knew it would be one of those frightening but memorable days in Hawaii.

Just as Bradshaw has peaked in his mid-40s, success has stayed with the other central figures of this book. Doerner became the first surfer to ride the tube at Peahi, the fabled tow-in spot on Maui, while adding to his nearly mythical status on many other fronts. Tom Nellis and Trevor Sifton still ride massive waves in their quiet, unassuming way. Mark Cunningham is still the most respected bodysurfer in the world, and Mike Stewart is so much more accomplished than any other bodyboarder, he should be placed in a separate category. Randy Rarick still surfs big Sunset and serves as the North Shore's voice of reason. Carol Philips still rides big Pipeline like no other woman on earth. And so many other central figures—Clyde Aikau, Brock Little, Richard Schmidt, James Jones, Owl Chapman, even Ricky Grigg and Peter Cole as they move into their 60s—remain prominent. Foo's death shocked the surfing world, as did the big-wave fatalities involving Todd Chesser, Donnie Solomon and Jim Broach in recent years. But in the wake of many tears and considerable soul-searching, the lure of the ocean is the final word. Nothing in the world can replace the satisfaction of leaving the water after a good session, and the feeling never goes away.

I figure I've spent more than three years of my life on the North Shore since my first visit in 1974, enough to see some incredible things. Special acknowledgement goes to the Keaulanas, the Hos, the McNamaras, Johnny Boy Gomes, Tony Moniz, Derek Ho, Sunny Garcia, Shane Dorian, Ross Williams and the other contemporary geniuses of all-around Hawaiian surfing, and to such less-recognized talents as Terry Ahue, Dennis Gouveia, Mel Pu'u, David Cantrell, Kerry Terukina, Dennis Pang, Archie Kalepa, Jeff Johnson ... an endless list, really, of surfers who truly distinguish themselves in island waters. I've always felt they should be earning huge salaries from their surfing alone—because in all of sports, nothing compares to taking a 20-foot drop, pulling into the tube over a mass of sharp, unforgiving coral, and emerging unscathed. For sheer courage and athletic ability, I'll stack that up against anything you can name.

A word about wave size: the Hawaiian scale (measured from trough to peak, before cresting) is used in all cases. If you see "4 to 6 feet," think 10-foot faces; "10-to-12" means

20-foot drops on the sets. I used to resent this curious system; it accurately gauges the waves as they travel through open ocean, but ignores the actual face size when they arrive on shallow reefs and become fully vertical. But I have come to respect it for one reason. If you hear "20 feet" on the North Shore, you know you're approaching maximum rideable size. The term is not thrown around lightly. Go ahead and tell your friends back home about those all-time drops you took, but don't call them 20 feet around the North Shore. Not unless you've been one of those fearless souls at big Waimea or out on the distant reefs.

As for my own surfing, let's just say that when the waves start pushing 10 feet, I get this tremendous urge to make a sandwich. For years I rode fiberglass bodyboards with skegs, enabling me to make long, sweeping bottom turns, which to me is what Hawaiian surfing is all about. More recently I've concentrated on bodysurfing, inspired by the talent and companionship of Cunningham and Stewart. But hey—nothing special. If I had to sum up my status on the North Shore, I'd be a friendly little goat turd, turning gray in the afternoon sun.

Special thanks to Randy Rarick, Bernie Baker, Jack Shipley, Pete Johnson, Rick Williams and a host of lifeguards for their expert advice, and to my employers at the *San Francisco Chronicle*, who hired me as a vacation-replacement back in '73. That was an 8-month gig that gave me the winter off, and the chance to make my first Hawaiian trip. Thanks also to Jack Pritchett, Cal Porter and Lon Porter, with whom I've shared 35 years of big-wave California surfing; to my dear Martha, who got the stoke and is now an accomplished surf photographer, and to my parents, Beverly and Gordon, who always thought it was a good idea.

The Wave

The month of February 1986 was an unusually big one on the North Shore. I don't think I've ever seen a day like Wednesday the 5th, when 35-foot closeout waves pounded Waimea Bay in sunny, glorious, offshore-wind conditions. The most serious surfers on the planet watched the Bay that afternoon, looking for some hint that the place might be rideable, but it never came. Nobody went out.

I was keeping a chart of the daily swells, and in the week spanning February 10-17, the average set waves were 10, 15, 10, 25, 15, 25, 25 and 15 feet, invariably blown out by stormy weather. It was right about this time that Rich Stevens, my oldest friend and a longtime bodysurfing partner, decided to visit for a few days. Deep down, I was thinking, "No way we'll get in the water," but this was a special occasion. The Stevens and Jenkins families had sailed to Hawaii on the *S.S. Matsonia* in 1958, and this would be Rich's first time back. What the heck, I thought. He'll see the biggest waves of his life. That's something you never forget.

Back home in Sebastopol, California, Rich's longtime companion, Cheryl VeHorn, was a little concerned. "You're going bodysurfing in *Hawaii?*" she said. "Honey, you don't even have a will."

Kind of a scary little prophecy she had there.

I had rented a small, one-bedroom cottage, the #9 unit of Ke Iki Hale, just as I'd done annually since 1976. I had a warm relationship with the proprietor, Alice Tracy, and a special feeling about the place—as if in spirit, it belonged to me. It was a choice location, right between Waimea and Pipeline, with swaying palm trees and a long, beautiful beach.

Ke Iki had—and still has—a rather unsavory reputation. The shorebreak is among the most treacherous in the world, routinely killing two or three people on the average each winter. It doesn't take much, just one little slip into the danger zone no more than 30 feet from the beach. Comfortable shoreline drops off severely into deep water, and in any kind of size, it's certain death for anyone without experience in rough surf. Tourists, military men, bogus bodysurfers, football players... Ke Iki has claimed them all. You might get lucky if someone calls in for a helicopter rescue, but there isn't a lifeguard tower in sight.

Rich arrived on the 20th, and sure enough, the surf was pounding. We watched a small, hardy crew taking on 15-foot Pipeline that evening, and the following day we caught some nice bodysurfing over on the east side. Back home on Ke Iki, we marveled at how these titanic waves would be breaking *right* out front—the beach is generally about 50 yards wide— yet somehow subside on the gently sloping embankment before coming straight into the living room.

On the night of February 22, it came *all* the way in.

Rich and I should have taken our cue that evening. As darkness fell, under a full moon, we headed down to watch Pipeline—a little imbibed, as I recall. The Civil Defense had issued a high-surf warning for the north and west shores, and when we got to Pipe, the beach had narrowed down to almost nothing. Suddenly, out of nowhere, an onrushing wall of whitewater sent us scurrying for cover. Rich, who always had the quicker reactions, scrambled up onto the bluff. I made a break but got completely drenched, head to foot. As we walked home, laughing heartily, I looked like some pathetic shipwreck survivor.

By 11 p.m., whitewater was beginning to splash gently against the Ke Iki beachfront homes. The swell was pushing 30 feet, and some of the residents were awake, getting a little more nervous all the time. I was sound asleep in the bedroom. Rich had knocked off, too, on a single bed in the adjoining room. We didn't have a clue as to what was coming.

Oceanographers have researched the phenomenon known as "rogue" waves. "Non-negotiable," as they're called by sailors and merchant seamen. They seem to show up without warning, the unlikely convergence of waves from two separate trains. If they are exactly in synch, they combine into one horrific monster. There wasn't much research on this particular wave, because it arrived in the middle of the night. But it was a rogue, baby. It was wild.

At around 11:50 p.m., it happened. WHAM! Unlike every other wave that night, this one hit the beach with a full head of steam, as if it had *just* broken. Its force blew open the wall next to Rich's bed and he shot into the outdoors, still aboard his mattress and not fully awake. He was riding the wave, quite literally, and he wound up under the laundry lines near the parking lot, some 50 feet away. The loyal mattress was still with him, and his only injury was a substantial welt in the middle of his back.

"The first thing I realized was sound," Rich told me later. "I didn't hear water, I heard the house breaking, just a tremendous crunching sound. Then — slowly, somehow — I was embroiled in water. I didn't know I was moving. I thought I was just being pummeled, right there. It didn't occur to me that I was traveling."

Oh, but he was. Right through the narrow walkway separating #9 and the larger, adjacent building. The bed frame got wedged in between, "but me, the box spring and the mattress took off," Rich said. "I remember being on my back, and my feet were up over my head, like I was doing a reverse somersault. But I never quite finished it; I was just suspended in that position.

"I knew I was underwater. It was that familiar feel: hold your breath and wait until the chaos subsides. Somehow, I had copped a good breath. I even had that feeling you get when you're awakened from a deep sleep, like, 'Wow, I was really out, wasn't I?' And that's the only thought I had, until I realized I was gonna need a breath real soon. Not panic, but Stage One. I need a breath."

And then it was over. Rich was finally ejected off the mattress onto cement. When he stood up, saltwater flooded off his sweat pants and T-shirt, and he could feel that distinctive North Shore sand, the pebble-sized grains, imbedded in his hair. "I started calling out for you," he said. "Alice came out of her place (on the inland side) and we were yelling, 'Bruce!' There was no answer. I still hadn't really grasped the fact that I'd been blown out of there. I didn't know *what* was going on. I mean, I lifted up the mattress to see if you were under *there.*"

I've always envied Rich a little, because while he has a clear memory of the event, I have none. The wave crashed through a plate-glass window and into my 12-by-15 bedroom, flinging me against the wall and transporting me into an unconscious state of shock. I have about a tenth-of-a-second worth of memory, sort of a blurred freeze frame, of the impact and the snapping of wood and the shattering of glass. And that's it. I'm told that a neighbor named Jim—"the unknown shadow ghost," Rich calls him—heard me crying out and rushed into the room, just long enough to pry me from underneath my bed. He bailed out quick, thinking there might be *another* wave, and that's when my consciousness begins. Standing there in a pile of wreckage, trying to sort it all out.

I must have been sleeping on my side, facing the inland wall. Otherwise, I would have no face. It would have been shredded by glass. I was wearing a sweatshirt, as there'd been a chill in the air, and I might even have pulled the blanket over my head. I do know this: When the wave got through with my bed, it was contorted beyond recognition. Everything was. I looked disbelievingly at the hideous re-arrangement of the place. The ceiling had collapsed; large pieces of furniture had moved from one room to another, if they were around at all.

And I didn't have an injury. I mean, not a scratch.

As I ventured into the living room, stepping over a mine field of sharp objects, I focused on the spot where Rich had been sleeping. Total devastation. I didn't just think he was dead, I *knew* he was. It was so heavy a realization that I went right past it. I had no trunks on. I need some trunks. Can't go outside without trunks. That's all I could think about. I couldn't even address the issue of Rich, and perhaps other fatalities.

He was pretty much thinking the same about me, and with waves steadily washing in at ankle level, Rich wasn't all that keen on going back up to the house. "I kept calling out," he said. "I was just about at the crisis point, where I'm *really* worried, when you went...'Yeah!'"

I staggered down the walkway and there we were, alive and trembling. Rich and Alice and I embraced, sort of laughing and crying at the same time. It was just so horrible—and so incredible.

By now, people were starting to emerge from their homes. That whole stretch of coastline was wasted, to the tune of about $500,000, and there were some tall tales. A washing machine and motorcycle were carried some 100 yards inland. One woman, Lee Roy, broke her kneecap when a glass door exploded under tons of whitewater and fell on top of her. She had to grab onto the refrigerator to keep from being sucked back out to sea, and she would eventually need major reconstructive surgery. In all, it was the most wave damage on the North Shore since the big-wave winter of '69. But only one place had to be completely torn down and rebuilt. Good old #9.

Once we realized the worst was over, summoning our courage to approach the beach and forage for our valuables, we saw an awesome sight: indescribably huge surf breaking in the moonlight, without a breath of wind in the palm trees, and a clear, star-filled sky. This is when Tommy Nellis entered the picture.

Nellis, a North Shore big-wave rider and shaper for nearly 20 years, had been in Honolulu that night. He lives just behind the Ke Iki Hale units, and he arrived to find his shop completely flooded, destroyed. "It was maybe 20 minutes after the wave hit," he said. "We've all seen the water come up and into our yards. And we say OK, we're gonna have to clean it up again. But there was *no* call for that wave. None at all."

Just how big was it? I figured Nellis would be the right man to ask. He's conservative in his wave-size judgment, and he's been out on 30-foot days at Waimea. His estimate—and he wasn't kidding—100 feet.

"I was watching those waves in the moonlight," he said. "Those were the biggest fucking waves I ever saw, Bruce, and they were nowhere *near* as big as the one that went through your house. They were 70 feet if they were a foot. Because I've seen 40, OK? I know what 40 feet looks like. I don't want to call 'em 80, so I'll call 'em 70 [laughter]. Those waves were breaking out where the whales swim. They were phenomenal creatures. I was scared *shitless.* I ran back to my house four or five times and got soaked in the process. This lasted until around 2 a.m., before it started dropping. Without a doubt the biggest surf since '69."

Now, you're not going to get too far with "100 feet" around the North Shore. That's a little much. Those who saw the '69 surf generally call it 40-50 feet, maybe 60 on the outside, and that swell destroyed four houses on Ke Iki. But Nellis is no fly-by-night source, and I heard him out. "I say it without hesitation," he went on. "I mean, it picked up cars and threw 'em on the other side of Kam Highway. It knocked your fuckin' house down. Hey, nobody would be arrogant enough to say it was a 100-foot wave, right? But I don't feel belittled by saying it, and if somebody gives me shit about it, hey—they weren't standing there watching it. I was there. And it was focused right *exactly* in front of your house."

I don't remember much about the rest of that night, except that we found a fair amount of stuff—just about all of the cash, in fact—and that a friendly group of New Zealand surfers put Rich and me up for the night. Neither one of us slept much. We couldn't get our minds off the wave, the destruction, the *consequence*, and the fact that we had somehow been spared. At one point, very late, Rich began sobbing. I reached over and grabbed his hand. I was just staring at the ceiling, seeing nothing.

The following morning, when Rich called Cheryl back home, she didn't recognize him. The tone of his voice, the phrasing, everything was different. We were both in a private little zone for several days, and as that first morning broke, we just wanted to assemble our tortured belongings and get out of there. My rental car had made it through the night, and we headed into Waikiki for two days before Rich caught a flight home.

"I remember saying, 'Rich, you're in worse shape than you know,'" Cheryl said. "I was really concerned, thinking these guys are over there functioning, walking around in traffic, but they are in shock."

It's funny, as we drove away from the North Shore that morning, the Eddie Aikau Invitational contest was going off in 20-foot surf at Waimea Bay. It would be four years before they held another Eddie, making it an even bigger deal in retrospect. Months later, when I saw the contest on videotape, I couldn't believe I'd missed it. But we drove right by. I swear, the waves looked small.

"We just needed a whole new setting," said Rich. "I remember when we got into town, I decided to review the Waikiki bars [laughter]. Just cast myself out there. See if anyone was talkin' about the wave."

They were. To this day, when I mention it to surfers on the North Shore, they ask, "Are you the guy who rode the mattress?" It's just a shame that it happened during the night, because it will never become part of the North Shore's surfing folklore. The more I think about it, the more I believe that, realistically, it was among the biggest waves ever to break on the shorelines of the Pacific.

Most of my friends were shocked by this development. Just about everyone else said, "Wow, guess you won't be going *there* again," with an elbow to the ribs and a chortle. But I looked at that night as a blessing, a magical and cherished event, a beginning. And it most certainly was. I had always believed in the higher order of things, that all events have a purpose, but now the message had been delivered first-hand. I wasn't in that house by accident. There was nothing "random" about my survival. I didn't know quite how to execute this new life I'd been given, but I figured it would be a pretty fine ride. And it would definitely be different. You don't get an opportunity like that and just hang it on a shelf somewhere.

When I returned for my eighth consecutive year on the baseball beat that spring, I was already considering new directions. Other writers scoffed and chided me, "You'd never give up a gig this good," but I was gone the following spring. I ventured into a book project, the life of my late father, musician Gordon Jenkins. I all but dropped out of sportswriting for a couple of years, and it was only through the patience and generosity of the *Chronicle* people, who had known me 13 years, that I was allowed to remain on the staff. Now, I hope the association never ends. They are like family.

In the winter of 1987-88, I was back on the North Shore. I spent nearly three months there. Occasionally I'd stop by #9, where they were just applying the finishing touches to the reconstruction job. (Alice didn't take any chances this time; she built the thing on 10-foot cement pilings.) And as fate would have it, I was the first person to stay in the rebuilt #9. I just wanted one night there, and Alice picked up the tab. Since then, on solo ventures, I invariably check in for a week or so. There's nothing strange or masochistic about my feelings for the place. I just know that it felt good then, and it still does. It feels just fine.

Ken Bradshaw

Ken Bradshaw stopped by for an interview one night and stayed five hours. He would have stayed longer, but it was getting late. Something just clicked between us right away, and it triggered an evening of rare insight into the North Shore and its players. In 20 years of interaction with the greatest stars of baseball, basketball, the NFL, you name it, this might have been the most interesting interview I've had.

Know this, by way of introduction: Bradshaw was brutally honest—it's the only way he knows—but never bitter, cruel or mean-spirited. While many of his statements were critical, they were spoken in a tone of amazement. Clear-eyed, animated and polite, Bradshaw simply laid down the law of North Shore surfing, at least as it exists in his mind. And one thing became obvious: It's not about hatred, rivalries or making enemies on the North Shore. It's a matter of style. Ken Bradshaw respects everyone who rides waves of this magnitude. It's their *style* he sometimes can't understand.

And if you challenge him, get him mad, push him a little too far…wow, that's a bad idea.

Bradshaw reminded me greatly of Howie Long, the Los Angeles Raiders' defensive tackle: well-spoken, tremendous presence, gentlemanly, yet a savage competitor when necessary. Ken also has an unusually large head, which you'll notice on Howie. And when this guy walks into a room, he takes charge. A herd of wild buffaloes could charge the coffee table,

19

and Bradshaw would retain command.

This is a man who has taken bites out of surfboards, just to make a point. He's been known to paddle up to another surfer—someone who has flagrantly broken the code of ethics—and simply rip out a fin with his bare hands. If an old-fashioned brawl is the last alternative, Bradshaw couldn't be more ready. "If it comes to that, I am going to survive," he says. "Ken Bradshaw *will* survive. I don't care what you do, who you bring, or how many. I will match whatever you give me."

Considering that Bradshaw rides the biggest, most fright-ening waves in the world, it is nothing short of amazing that he grew up in Texas. It's one thing to make the jump from California—countless big-wave riders have done that, from Buzzy Trent to Sam Hawk to Richard Schmidt—but Texas? "It all comes down to desire," he says in his earnest, high-pitched voice, without a trace of an accent. And if you grew up the only son of Kenneth Bradshaw, Sr., desire counted big. "My father's story is way more radical than my story," he says. "I had this *thing*. It wasn't a father, it was a god."

The elder Bradshaw's roots were in Texas oil, and he established a successful pipe-fitting business that had the fam-ily moving to Florida and Alabama (three years each) and finally Houston during Kenny's childhood. "To find my dad, you had to look in three or four places. He was vice president of the corporation. He was mayor of a little town called Spring Branch. He was a captain in the Houston sheriff's department. He did everything. Really a tough individual, too. A couple of years ago, he was walking to the store at night when a young black guy jumped him. Wanted his money. My dad goes, 'You fuck with me, you're fuckin' with death.' And he's 74 years old! The guy laughed and punched him, and my father kicks him in the nuts, knocks him into the street, bends his arm back, and holds him there until the police show up. He's radical. Military radical. He was in special forces in Germany. He acted as a deaf-mute on reconnaissance mis-sions; he'd go behind the lines as a driver with an American guy who could speak German. He's been shot… let's see, twice in the back, once in the stomach, once in the knee. This is the kind of guy I grew up with. I mean, I *couldn't* grow up with him."

Not when Kenny chose surfing over football. He'd been an all-city linebacker in high school, probably bound for greatness at some big university, "and it was fun, no doubt about it," he recalls. "I loved head-huntin'. You know, roving monster man, just search and destroy." He was a formidable 5-10, 165 pounds in the 10th grade (compared to 6-0, 185 today), and he probably could have written his own ticket by his senior year. But when Kenny discovered the waves at Surfside, Texas, near Galveston, he realized that nothing else really mattered in life. He had found his calling. "It was about a 75-mile drive from Houston, and my sister started taking me down there when I was about 13. People give Texas a hard time, but there was a lot of surf then. Not fantastic, but big, long, mushy peaks, where you could get some paddling experience and wave knowledge. There was no intimidation factor, no overpowering situations, so I did nothing but conquer the waves. I conquered every wave I came across in Texas, so that's all I knew.

"I'd be out surfing all day—just 10 straight hours in the water. My sister literally had to come out and say, 'We're leaving without you.' I got so into surfing a couple of summers, my parents just couldn't handle it. I didn't want to play football any more, and for them, that was it. We had a big war. I ran away from home twice."

The second time was for good. Bradshaw, now 17, had graduated from nine-foot boards down to seven-footers in a very short time. He entered a Surfside contest; reached the semifinals. He had conquered Texas, and he was ready for California.

Imagine his good fortune—it was the winter of 1969-70, one of the biggest in recorded history.

"I found a place in Encinitas and spent that whole winter surfing Swami's, Windansea and Trestles. It was huge, incredible. That was my first winter in California, so that's what I thought surfing was. It's big. Every day's big! I'm out at Swami's, and I'm out in the kelp beds! This is great! By Christmas, I was surfing as well as most of the guys around: Cheer Critchlow, Alf Laws, Tom Ortner. In any size I could get my hands on. It was a whole new world, and I was on fire."

Eventually, he caught wind of the real California: 0-1 foot, with possible 2-foot sets. Blown out by noon. Interminable boredom. Find a job, and fast. Catch the surf movies, and dream of Hawaii. "I was 19, it was the winter of '71-72, and there was no surf. I was living alone in an apartment, just ready to break out. I figured, I've got to at least *see* Hawaii. It had a real mystique then. Everybody comes over here now, but then, you'd see guys get on a plane to Hawaii, and they wouldn't return."

Bradshaw arrived in the spring of '72, and he did return to California, briefly—just in time to see the 1972 World Contest at Ocean Beach. That was a mind-blowing event, featuring the likes of David Nuuhiwa, Larry Bertleman, Jimmy Blears (a new acquaintance from Hawaii) and the astounding Michael Ho, reaching the finals at the age of 13. "That was it," said Bradshaw. "About two weeks after that, I packed up for Hawaii —it was the second week of October—and I came to stay."

Bradshaw found a place in Kahala, took a town job and hitch-hiked to the North Shore when he could. "If you didn't make money to survive, you didn't surf," he recalls. "I didn't care if it took me two years before I could go surfing. I knew it was out there. My first experience...you remember it like you remember your first girl. I paddled out at Sunset with a bunch of hot guys out—I remember Sam Hawk, definitely—and it was about 8 feet. I had my California surfboard, and I'm going real fast, *wow*, and I start my turn...and the tail was just too thin. First time I'd ever been in a real tube in Hawaii. The wave just passed me by and snuffed me. I came up, and I was *so* stoked. I mean, the power didn't bother me; nothing bothered me. It was just being in Hawaii, being able to do it."

Bradshaw probably inherited more from his father than he realized. He went after his surfing with a raging aggression, driven to be the best, and unlike so many of today's hotshots, he carried deep respect for the North Shore: its lore, its legends, the surfers who came before him, and the very real mystique surrounding places like Pipeline and Waimea Bay. The sight of a Greg Noll, Jose Angel or Peter Cole would stop Bradshaw in his tracks, because these were the pioneers, the ground-breakers. In his book, *Da Bull: Life Over the Edge*, Noll wrote, "Every big-wave rider I've met is a radical individual. Ken Bradshaw has got the spark. He's intense, he wants it and he's willing to give up something for it if he has to. Ken Bradshaw spent many years riding big waves before he got any recognition for it. You have to love what you're doing to go out there and do it when the bleachers are empty."

In that same book, Ricky Grigg noted, "Kenny is one of the few surfers at Waimea who does it like we used to, with the same fanatical vigor. The guy claws his way into a wave. There are other guys out there with lots of style, but Kenny has true grit. It's something that comes out of thunder and lightning."

Bradshaw's big-wave initiation came on a day in 1976 when the Bay was pushing 30 feet and more. "I went out with Roger Erickson," he recalled. "All morning long it was closing out, 40 feet. Eddie [Aikau] tried to warn me. 'Oh, brudda Brad, you don't go out when it's this big, brah.'

"But there's waves between the sets that are unreal," Bradshaw told him.

"No, brah. When the waves are hitting the bath house [up where the beach meets grass], you don't paddle out."

Bradshaw barely knew Erickson then, but they took on the Bay together. "We stayed out three hours, and I got three or four waves. Then Eddie and Kimo Hollinger came out, and a huge set came in and caught everybody. That was Kimo's last day. A rogue set came in, totally out of time, out of sync."

Hollinger nearly drowned that day. He was pushed over toward the diving rock, synonymous with disaster on a big day, and it took a human chain of seven or eight Hawaiian watermen, clinging tenuously to the rocks, to haul him out of the water.

"He didn't surf again for like five years, anywhere," said Bradshaw. "I was amazed. But I'm like 22, just amped out of my mind, going (desperately) 'I'm going back out there.' And there's Kimo. 'I don't *care*,' I'm saying. You think I get fired-up now, you should have seen me in the '70s. I was a tyrant. I look at these guys now and think, 'You *might* have it.' Boy, I *had* it. I was hell-bent. I'd *kill* somebody who got in my way."

And he damn near did. Word quickly spread that Bradshaw was not only fearless, tackling 15-foot Sunset and 25-foot Waimea at every opportunity, but a little bit nasty. Not surprisingly, some of the local boys were offended by this brash young warrior. There were violent confrontations, both in and out of the water. "I really got into it with these two guys at Sunset once, and when it was over, one of them said, 'Wow, man, you're *serious*, aren't you?' I said hey, this is my life. You're the one who made it serious, not me."

Mike Latronic, who has shared countless big days with Bradshaw at Sunset, describes him as "really smart, an intelligent guy, and very polite. Ninety-nine percent of the time, he's a really cool guy. But if you cross him in the water, he turns into an animal."

I asked Bradshaw if he really did take a bite out of somebody's surfboard.

"Oh, that's commonplace for me. Even today."

"Is that your ultimate statement?" I asked. "I mean, that's a serious statement."

"It is. As much of a brute and bull as people see me, I don't do something unless it's really called for. I wouldn't recommend somebody using the 'F' word at me when he's in the wrong. I wouldn't suggest that."

"Biting a board...that takes some strength," I said.

"It takes *desire*. Four-ounce surfboards are really easy, though. The six-ounce ones [laughter]...my teeth were loose the other day. Breaking fins is probably more effective, because then they have to leave the water. Tri-fins are real easy. You just bend 'em right off. If you feel bad about it later, you can give 'em 15 bucks. That's what it costs to put 'em back on. But at least you got the guy out of there."

Bradshaw didn't appreciate the Australian-South African invasion of the North Shore in the '70s. Not in the slightest. "I was really against what all those guys stood for. I didn't like Michael Peterson. I didn't appreciate Rabbit Bartholomew, Shaun Tomson or Ian Cairns. Out of the group, Mark Richards was the only one that seemed like a normal kind of guy. I just didn't appreciate anybody coming over here, having no respect for the people who live here, and just burning for waves, jockeying for position. I think the people who live here should get more respect than the jerk-offs who come in for 30, or even 90 days a year. They got their friggin' contests, OK, go out and surf in that. But I don't want to see those contest tactics on a day-to-day basis. I called bullshit on it. Still do. But in those days, I was really bad about it.

"I remember Michael Peterson at Sunset, years ago, and he kept hounding me for waves, saying things, just paddling right in front of me. Finally I just took off behind him, ran up his back, grabbed him by the head, and just [two explosive, cracking sounds]!! Just blasted him.

"Tom Curren was another. I started off hoping the guy was gonna be unreal. I figured if he looks like he needs some help, maybe I can do something for him. Well, first time I surfed with him that winter, at Rocky Point, he burned me three times in a row. He was *so* like all the other guys. Then we're at Sunset... and see, I have a problem. I have to get angry before I can get like them. And to get waves, I have to *become* like them. So therefore, I don't like myself, and I don't like anything that's going on at that point. So he's diggin' and hustlin', and I was *not* liking him. Finally I catch this wave, and the northwest bowl's coming up, kind of mushy, and I see this guy paddling for it ahead of me. I'm thinking, I don't believe this guy. It's Tommy. What's he doing? So I go right by him, do a cutback, and he drops in *behind* me.

"That was it. That set me off. I paddled back out, went straight for him, and just [violent, animal-like sound]. Ran right into him. Knocked him off his board. He came up, and I said, 'You little turd, who the hell do you think you are?' That sort of thing. I sent him in. Literally. He went in. And he never did it again! But see, that's the sad thing about it. People will act like three-year-old kids, just push, push, push, to find out how much they can get away with. Until mommy and daddy stop them, they will take and take and take."

Bradshaw may be a tad more mellow these days, but he finds the situation just as pitiful. "A big part of surfing Hawaii is being a water man. That gets so overlooked by this new world of surfers coming in. The Japanese, the Asian world, the Latin American surfers, they come in with absolutely no understanding, no respect, no regard for consequence or the people who've come before. You heard about the guy at Laniakea, the Brazilian guy who bled to death in the water. He couldn't swim in! And we lost a Japanese guy at Haleiwa. They're so paranoid —the board's lost, they've got to make that swim, they've got a hole in them... hey, if you don't know what you're doing, you're gonna die. And they did! Simply died.

"The sad irony to the whole thing, in a sick way, I almost wish it would happen more, just so people would get respect. But these guys get away with murder in the water, and it's funny, the culture is reflected in their personalities. The polite, reserved, organized thought of the Japanese is far more tolerable than the Latin machoism, most-aggressive-wins. The Brazilians surf the way they drive. The Japanese are just oblivious—to problems, situations, scenarios they could avoid if they just got out of the way for a minute. But they're oblivious. They just freeze.

"See, we learned from surf movies in the old days, from the guys who would come back with stories. You didn't paddle out at places like Sunset or Waimea, or even Haleiwa, because you had so much respect built in. The first thing you say isn't, 'Looks pretty good today.' It's, 'Where does your board go if you lose it?' Nobody thinks about that, with leashes. I'm so glad to have been brought up when they didn't exist.

"It's really sad, to think so many people surf today with absolutely no idea how to get *in* at a place. You see guys out at Sunset, just swimming out to sea. 'Where are you going?' you say. 'See that house? Head for that house and don't look back. Get into the whitewater, take your punishment and get out of here. Otherwise we'll still be lookin' at you an hour from now.'"

Bradshaw sees himself as sort of a Sunset caretaker. He watches everything that's going on, who's doing what, and he enjoys being called upon for advice — especially when things get hairy. Latronic recalled one long-ago afternoon when a 4-6-foot swell suddenly jumped to 10 feet and beyond, "and there were like 20 waves in the set. I let my board go, and the leash broke, and I'm just, 'Oh, no!' I started swimming out, and that was a mistake. I went under about four more waves, and just [sound of desperate, heaving breaths]...I'm gettin' scared. Finally Bradshaw says, 'Swim in! Go in!' He's just *bellowing*. I was scared to go in, because it was shallow, but you have to, and I learned that. It's the only way."

Bradshaw was showing Richie Collins around the North Shore in the winter of 1988-89, and that seemed like a contradiction. Collins, the tempestuous young Californian, has been quoted as saying, "I'm just too aggravated and stressed to be humble," and "A lot of times, if a guy even looks at me wrong, I psych myself out so bad that I want to destroy him instantly." But Bradshaw saw some admirable qualities in Collins: talent, desire, and an almost maniacal disdain for distractions (he shaved his head once, partly so he'd be less attractive to women). "Richie is pure surf," says Bradshaw. "He's got the energy and the heart to surf big waves. The only thing he's got against him is that he's young and he's arrogant. But he's the closest one I've seen recently to the way I was, just pure surf."

Bradshaw's advice to Collins: "You've got an image. Fine. But with that comes a lot of flak. Make sure the image you get, that's the one you want them to have. Because right now you're the tough guy, the bad-dude surfer. I guarantee you, Johnny Boy Gomes wants to be the baddest bad guy. And right now *you're* the baddest bad guy, as far as the media is concerned. But in reality, we all know you're *not* the baddest bad guy. *Johnny's* the baddest bad guy [laughter]. And Johnny *wants* to be that guy."

Johnny Boy. There's a name to stop any North Shore conversation. I've seen a lot of great surfers glide past me over the years—Gerry Lopez, Dane Kealoha, Nat Young, Wayne Lynch —but Johnny Gomes is the only one who actually seemed more powerful than the wave. He tries impossible things out there, insane things, and pulls them off, with one of the most vicious attitudes ever seen in the water. I saw him rip the fin off a guy's board, right in front of me at Log Cabins, and the look on his face was unforgettable. After that, I wouldn't even think of paddling for a wave within 50 yards of him. Mike Stewart, a friend and admirer of Johnny Boy, believes that his attitude is *so* severe, he actually mellows out the crowd. There's just no competing with this guy; only the foolish would attempt it.

"He's a dangerous man," said Latronic. "He paddles out at V-land one day and says, 'OK. Nobody moves, nobody gets hurt [laughter].' He's actually a really nice guy. You just don't want to be on his angry side."

The story is related to Bradshaw. "Johnny Boy…you know, what an unbelievably fantastic surfer he is. I have a hard time saying this, but I haven't seen anyone surf Sunset as good as Johnny Boy is right now. I mean, there was Barry Kanaiaupuni, Jeff Hakman, Shaun Tomson, Ian, Richards, guys like that, but this is Johnny's time. I hope he can sustain it, because he could have problems. Johnny's a time bomb. He's programmed to destruct. I talk to Johnny. I'm one of the few people who do. Not 'Oh, Johnny, that was such a good ride.' Real things. I tell him, whatever the sport is, keep it for life. See what you get out of it. I tell him, stop giving everybody a hard time, because you're *way* ahead of them. I don't want to see you burn out or fade away."

Bradshaw stops for a moment. "There I go again, Ken the Philosopher. I'm real bad about that. But I'm trying to give you a very real view of these people and the way I see them. I don't say anything I can't live with or will regret. I look at people and their surfing, and see if there's something holding them back."

Owl Chapman, for instance, completely baffles Bradshaw. Owl is a living legend on the North Shore, a man who surfed second-reef Pipeline backside when it was considered beyond the limits of good sense; a man who has surfed big Sunset as much as anyone. But the *style*. Bradshaw just can't get over it.

"He rides a 12-foot board everywhere he goes, and that's such a mistake," Bradshaw said in '89. "The other day, I saw an older surfer come up to Owl, real impressed, and he asks [breathlessly], 'God, Owl, what do you ride when it gets big?' And that's it. That's exactly the true statement. What will Owl ride when it gets big? It's just human nature; if you ride a certain board in 12-foot surf, you *have* to have a bigger board in 20 feet, so you can feel good about yourself. So you can paddle it better. Owl wants more paddling ability; well, he won't get any more than he already *has*. If you drive a Formula One car around the streets all the time, and all of a sudden you're on the track...you're lost. You've got to feel the rush of your equipment, the stuff you've saved for *that* moment.

"I say to him, Owl, you're too good of a surfer to ride that board. You're too good! So, OK, the psychologist in me does it again. But he's riding this big thing, so he can catch every wave at Sunset, so he can feel good about himself. I remember the time he lost his favorite Dick Brewer board in the channel at Sunset, just lost it at sea, and he was so in shock. He shaped for everybody else, but he wouldn't shape his *own* sufboards. Owl Chapman will not shape his own surfboards! Now, does that say something about the man? He didn't surf for a month, because Brewer was out of town that long. He got all weirded out, meanwhile shaping other people's boards left and right."

On the 15th of January, the first day of my six-week 1990 visit, I ran into Owl at the pizza joint above Sunset. I wanted to interview him—not to get a reaction on Bradshaw, but because he belonged. "Don't want to do no book," he said, with sort of a scary-brilliant expression. "I'm into shaping. Shaping and surfing. Low-key."

He asked who I'd interviewed. I rattled off some of the names.

"What'd Bradshaw say?"

"Said a lot of things," I answered. "He's kind of down on your board."

Owl paused for a moment, then looked me straight in the eye and said, "I've ridden more big waves than any man in the world—dead or alive." And as he walked out the door, he said, "You take it easy. Good luck on the pages."

Bradshaw would love to be one of those backside Pipeline standouts. "I have a lot of respect for what Pipeline is," he says. "The problem I have is the people. There are distinct personality traits that go with each break. You'll find the people who surf Sunset are older, more regimented, more experienced, more into the long-term lifestyle. People who surf Pipeline are more for the moment, nervous, amped-out; *right now*, instead of goal-oriented. And therefore very unpredictable. Like the break itself. It's funny, the break almost creates the man. Pipeline is a 3-5-second ride, you're in, you're out, it's over. Sunset is like a lifetime. You gotta understand it, build on it, say, 'This swell does this. And this swell does this. And if I sit here, this will happen to me.' I mean, I'm sorry, Pipeline guys—and hey, the top guys are always exceptions. Guys like Gerry Lopez and the Ho brothers. But Pipeline is a young, arrogant, adolescent crowd. Snappy. Pissed off. If I go there, I'm gonna get straightened out on half my waves for no reason, and I'll get into a fight or a yelling contest. Hey, the regular surfer there, if he's in the wave and he thinks he's gonna get his picture taken, he'll drop in on *anybody* at *any* time for *any* reason."

And then, ladies and gentlemen, there is Waimea Bay.

For years, the Bay was reserved for the big boys, the true emperors of the North Shore. Then came the Eddie Aikau contest, with its $55,000 first prize, and people got a little crazy. Big-wave riding made a comeback and a lot of frauds got involved, cluttering up the break when they had no business being out there. "It's turned into a madhouse," says Bradshaw. "There's a whole new crowd at 12-15 feet, all these guys thinking they're gonna get rich and be hotshot big-wave riders. But when Waimea is *really* Waimea, there can be 25-30 guys out and it's still in the hands of the people who want it. And you've got to *want* Waimea."

Nobody wanted it more than Quiksilver, the Aikau contest sponsor, but for three full winters after the inaugural event in '86, Waimea didn't cooperate. At least a dozen surfers theorized that if Quiksilver dropped its name from the logo (the Quiksilver Eddie Aikau Invitational), the waves would come around immediately. But no such luck. The wait became interminable. The Bay got more crowded. And committed surfers like Bradshaw got increasingly annoyed at the list of 33 invitees. "Don't get me wrong," he said, "Quiksilver has helped countless surfers over the years, and now they're attempting to put something back into big-wave riding. But unfortunately, as in life, there is bad along with the good."

This was Bradshaw's evaluation of the field going into the contest, which finally went off in January of '90 (see final chapter for an account of that epic day):

Tom Carroll and Tom Curren: "Carroll is more capable than Curren. I have yet to see Curren in anything over 20 feet. I've yet to *hear* of him being out in 20 feet. I know he's a great surfer, but what's he doing in a contest that's 20 feet and above? Tom Carroll's doing it because he's that good of a surfer, and he wants to arrive at the next level."

Ross Clarke-Jones: "Real go-getter, he wants to do it, but he's never seen 20-plus surf. He got a lot of play in the Billabong contest ('86) at Waimea, because a couple of guys bailed out and nearly drowned, and he looked better than most of the unknowns. But that was a 15-18-foot day, fun, with a big set or two in the morning."

Gary Elkerton: "He's got a lot more enthusiasm and drive than he used to have, and he's older, trying to get to the next level. But questionable."

Hawaiians Marvin Foster, Hans Hedemann, Derek Ho, Michael Ho and Marty Hoffman: "Marvin has proven himself. Hans has. Derek is questionable. Derek doesn't seem to like it. I mean, he can do it because he's that good and he's been asked to, but he doesn't seem to like it. Michael Ho will go for it, for sure. Marty Hoffman has proven it through the years."

Cheyne Horan and Rabbit Bartholomew: "Cheyne would like to do it. He's got the equipment and is gearing toward it. He's like Rabbit. More qualified, if you ask me. Rabbit doesn't put in the time, preparing himself. At some point you just have to get the equipment and say, 'I want to surf 20-foot waves.'"

Clyde Aikau, Bradshaw, Darrick Doerner, Roger Erickson, Mark Foo, Keone Downing, James Jones: "Automatics."

Dane Kealoha: "Interesting. I don't know. I'd like to see what Dane would do. I've never seen Dane on a big day. But he definitely deserves to be in there."

Brian Keaulana: "Best big-wave rider from the Makaha side, no doubt about it."

Titus Kinimaka, from the North Shore of Kauai: "Just say that he surfs Hanalei at 18 feet. I mean, the guy is a *good* surfer. He's one of the unknowns in Hawaii that needs more notoriety, because he's unbelievable."

Wes Laine: "East Coast surfer. Potential. Never seen him in a wave over 20 feet."

Brock Little: "Young, up and coming, probably will do real good. Wants it real bad. He's put some time in, especially for a young guy. He's really doing it."

Waimea shorebreak

The author's rented cottage after a "rogue" wave struck the North Shore at midnight. "I was sleeping in that bed. I don't know how I made it out alive."

A gallery of big-wave riders: four of the all-time best at Waimea Bay

Ken Bradshaw

Michael Grosswendt

Roger Erickson

Michael Grosswendt

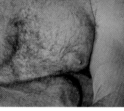

Mark Foo

Michael Grosswendt

Darrick Doerner

Jenkins

Ken Bradshaw in his element, when most would be watching from the beach

Bradshaw off the bottom at gigantic Waimea

Mark Foo, Alec Cooke, James Jones and J.P. Patterson went under this monstrous wave, probably the biggest ever faced by surfers, at Waimea Bay in 1985. That's Jones' 10-foot board, looking very insignificant.

The Mark Foo bottom turn, in ideal conditions

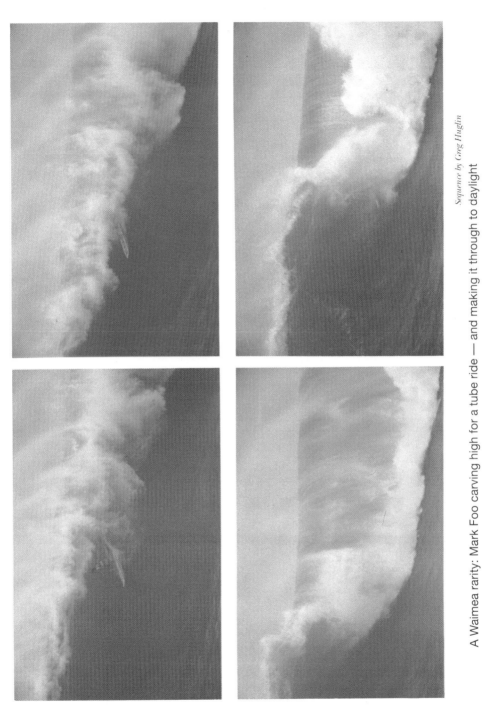

Sequence by Greg Huglin

A Waimea rarity: Mark Foo carving high for a tube ride — and making it through to daylight

Gordinho

Legends of Hawaii: Gerry Lopez at Pipeline

Gordinho

James Jones at Waimea

Barry Kanaiaupuni at Sunset

Ricky Grigg at Sunset

Killer set at Pipeline. No takers.

Alec Cooke, paddling into 30-foot, outer-reef Pipeline in January, 1985. "He's got a lousy reputation," said photographer Warren Bolster, who shot from a helicopter. "But I don't care what anyone says — this was the heaviest thing I've ever seen."

Huge, perfect Laniakea: The North Shore at its best.

Clyde Aikau (flanked by Owl Chapman and Brian Keaulana) after winning the 1986 Quiksilver contest.

Dane Kealoha

Michael Ho

Tony Moniz: "Of all the contenders from Hawaii, with the exception of Hans and Michael Ho, Tony is probably the most competitive."

Aaron Napoleon, Mickey Neilsen, Hawaii: "Aaron's an interesting choice. He's obviously a Quiksilver rider, very good surfer, unbelievable heart. I can't help but wonder. I mean, how often have I seen Aaron Napoleon out there on a regular Waimea day? Same thing with Mickey Neilsen. Both have proven they can do it, but I've never really seen them out there. And I'm *on* it. I've probably only missed one good day out of the 14 years I've been surfing it avidly."

Bobby Owens, Dennis Pang, Hawaii: "Bobby has proven himself over the years. Dennis? Big Hawaiian surfer, North Shore surfer, lot of stoke, lot of drive, and becoming more regular out there. He'll definitely do it."

Martin Potter: "How come? I don't know why. I mean, the biggest I've seen Martin Potter surf is 15 feet. Maybe 18."

Mark Richards: "Won't ride the normal Waimea equipment. He'll try to ride a smaller board on a bigger wave. I like that. Among the ASP [professional circuit] guys, he's the best. If he's in town, he'll do it."

Richard Schmidt: "Always there. Shows a lot of heart, a lot of promise. He's there with Carroll, Hans, Michael Ho, Moniz. Solid."

Shaun Tomson: "Shaun'll go out, Shaun's good, and Shaun'll catch waves, and…Shaun will be Shaun. But he's not gonna be here for it."

Takao Kuga, Japan: Bradshaw saw his name, but forgot to make a comment.

You can't blame Quiksilver for seeking out the sport's best-known names, but the Aikau contest ignores and insults the Waimea underground. You get the feeling Eddie wouldn't have liked that. Bradshaw definitely doesn't.

"Two guys, Bill Sickler and Gary Speece, are so massively overlooked, it's sad," said Bradshaw. "Bill's in his early 40s; he and [Jeff] Hakman used to live together. He'll take off on just about anything that comes through. Tommy Nellis, definitely. Tony Roy. Speece is slowing down a little, due to his job and family, but in his time, Gary would take off on anything that moved."

Bradshaw spoke passionately about Charlie Walker, one of the real monsters of big-wave lore. He's won the major North Shore paddling races, such as the one from Sunset to Waimea, and they say he once sanded 51 boards in a single day. Some years ago, Leonard Brady photographed Walker doing the first recorded snapback in Waimea history; the shot shows him rocketing off the top of what looks like a 30-foot face. And he's about as deep as they come. In an interview once, Walker said, "I go down with the guys who are out. I go down with Eddie—every time I go out, I see him. I see life, I see death. I see every mistake I've made."

Bradshaw said he'd include Charlie Walker at the top of his list, "but he's lost it. Totally lost it. Alcohol and drugs. He became a casualty of his own insecurity. It got to the point where he destroyed himself. He's living on the beach some-where around here. Sometimes I see him on the roads, just walkin' around. In '83, I would have picked Charlie as my best backup. Now I'd pick Darrick Doerner. He's the only guy right now who really captures the kind of surfing I like to see."

(Walker, incidentally, made something of a comeback. Both Bradshaw and Doerner spoke of riding Sunset and Waimea with Charlie in the winter of '90-91. Beyond that, Walker's status is entirely his own.)

"Everybody talks about Mark Foo now, or Brock Little," Bradshaw went on. "They're not the surfer that Darrick is. He's going to be unique. He's more emotional, he does it for personal reasons. Doesn't care about magazines or sponsor-ship. He's a little like Eddie that way—and I mean, Eddie was *pure.* It was Waimea, and the biggest one, and he was directed, he was funneled. Nothing could sidetrack him. Wife, family, it didn't *matter.* Drugs, alcohol, it didn't *matter.*"

Bradshaw doesn't have much to do with Mark Foo.

Although he's run his own surfing and shaping business for years, Bradshaw considers himself a purist. He doesn't understand Foo's style, in or out of the water.

"On a big day at Waimea, communication is critical," Bradshaw said. "You don't say, 'Yeah, maybe.' You say, 'Go, Charlie! Go NOW!' Or, 'I'm gonna take it, too, just in case.' And the other guy: 'OK!' It's direct orders. Darrick and I have real good communication. There's only about four of us that do it. Mark's not in the game. Mark won't help anybody else, so he's not in it. And Charlie...Damn him! For burnin' out on me. Just really pisses me off. He and I would surf together all those years, from '74 to '86. I mean, this is a guy, if he said go, I wouldn't even look at the *wave*. I wouldn't *care* what the wave looked like. If Charlie thought I could make it, that's all I needed.

"I wish I had that with Roger [Erickson]. He works from an inner passion, I think. It's real interesting. He has to get completely inside himself, before he attacks. He's the Viet Nam vet [heavily decorated; Erickson went through hell six times over in combat], and he probably got *so* radical over there that he made it. And that's the way he approaches his surfing. He sits off to the side, just in turmoil, and then he suddenly comes into the picture and turns on. After about a half-hour, he splits, that's it. He's hot and cold, boy. But hey, when he's hot, he paddles in as deep as anybody, ever. I've seen him [lowering his voice, in awe], 'Oh, *go*, Rog.' I mean, he's *way* back. He's so unreal. He'll do it straight-out, and paddle back out laughing."

The fundamental differences between Bradshaw and Foo cover the entire surfing spectrum, especially their attitudes toward surfing the outer reefs—the distant cloudbreaks that only show up in 20-foot swells. Foo will take anything available—helicopters, boats, whatever—to get out there and ride. "And I think that's bullshit," says Bradshaw. "Mark really believes that modern technology is just the greatest thing in the world: the Zodiacs, the helicopters, the jet skis. But if you can't do it under your own power, you should question your-self: Should I be out there? Because it's not true surfing. If you got out there with a helicopter, and you don't trust your-self getting in, where does that leave you, Mark Foo? What if you have mechanical problems? If your brother's not there to pick up after you, then what?

"Mark doesn't have the same quest that I was on. His quest is fame and fortune, getting photographed. Mine was to ride big waves, and I didn't care if I got paid for it, ever. In the begin-ning, Mark wasn't a big-wave rider in anyone's eyes. He rarely surfed Sunset, and he wasn't at Waimea that much. All of a sud-den, he found a niche that people would pay attention to."

That may be oversimplifying it a bit, but on January 18, 1985, Foo *did* step to the front. He encountered what Brad-shaw called "the biggest wave I've ever seen a human being in the water for." Then he took off on a 30-footer— pretty much the outer limit—a few minutes later. Foo truly earned his niche that day at Waimea. Bradshaw, of course, was also involved. He remembers that day in crystal-clear detail.

"It was just getting bigger and bigger," said Bradshaw. "Richard Schmidt lost his board, and pretty soon everybody was going in. I was the only guy out. And I mean it was consis-tent: 18, 18, 20, 20, 18, 20 feet on the sets. Pretty soon, 20, 22, 22, 25. It was so west, so thick and gnarly... *big*, nasty things. I mean, 25 feet *easily*, and I got two or three of 'em. I could see Gary Speece on the beach. I could see his car and all these people, and I'm thinking, 'Wow, why doesn't anybody come out here?'"

The spectators included James Jones, one of the all-time greats at the Bay, a man who pioneered Waimea tube-riding in the late '70s, and the notorious Alec Cooke. Known commonly as Ace Cool—a nickname he actually encourages— Cooke has ridden and bodysurfed big Hawaiian waves for years. Regrettably, he's also made a spectacle of himself, trumpeting his courage at every opportunity. Although Cooke often backs up his talk with outrageous feats, he is widely ridiculed on the

North Shore for his staggering lack of humility. As a result, he generally acts as a party of one.

"Finally, I lost my board," Bradshaw went on. "I didn't have a leash. There were only 12-foot leashes then, nothing at all for Waimea. I swam for 45 minutes trying to get in."

This might have been one of Bradshaw's greatest accomplishments. If you're out there swimming, the idea is to approach the point rocks and glide swiftly in, timing your entry around the sets. But in big, consistent surf with a raging current pulling you in the opposite direction, this becomes a Herculean feat. Bradshaw approached the point twice, only to find himself trapped and forced to scramble back to the channel. As he described it, "I did three laps around the Bay." If you've ever seen the place going off at 25 feet, try to imagine yourself out there for an hour without a board or fins. It's almost inconceivable.

"That's just about the manliest thing I've ever seen done," said Tom Nellis, who was also on the beach. "That was *heavy*. It would have been real easy for the guy to just give up. But he finally got his chance, and he just stuck his head down and *beat* it for the beach. Insane."

Bradshaw said he found out later that Jones had been watching him the whole time. "As soon as I got in, he probably figured he could make it, and he paddled out. Then, all of a sudden Mark Foo shows up! And Alec Cooke! It's the Battle of the Big Balls!"

From that point on, said Bradshaw, "I probably had the most fun I've had at Waimea in years. I sat there and watched these guys dodge waves for the next 45 minutes. Pretty much what I'd been doing out there. It was so west, it would just heave up and [sucking in his breath dramatically] . . . BOOM! After about 45 minutes, this rogue set comes in. And I'm just, 'Wow...look at this *thing*. It's giant!' I'm jumping up and down on the beach like a little kid, going, 'These guys are history.'

"I mean, they're paddling over sets, like 25-30 feet, scratching over the tops like a bunch of guys at Sunset, and this thing's already *pitching* outside! It was Sickler and Speece and Owl Chapman and Charlie Walker, Peter Cole and myself, all standing on the beach, just not believing it. We were calling this wave 45 feet, conservative. It could have been over 50, who knows? There was so much whitewater, we couldn't tell what was going on. We were trying to find heads. Like, 'You seen 'em? Are they up yet? Are they dead?'"

Foo, Jones and Cooke went under that wave, and they all lived to tell about it. Most incredibly of all, Foo still had his board. "Those guys were so strung out, they were all hanging together in the middle of the bay," said Bradshaw. "Then the helicopter comes, the basket goes down, and James Jones [snaps fingers] . . . right into it. Just like that. Alec, the big macho man, you see him kind of, 'Naww.' And he starts to swim in. But not toward the [point] rocks. Oh, no. Absolutely no intellect as to what was going on around him. He was just like a guy at Sunset, going straight in. He got to the shore-break, and that was just about the most entertaining 20 minutes I've ever spent. We were takin' bets on Alec. He's dead. Just eat shit. We were so busy watching him, we weren't even watching Mark."

Which was a shame, because Foo took it upon himself to surf his way in. "I gotta hand it to him," said Bradshaw. "It was definitely a 30-foot wave, one of those middle-of-the-bay sets. To be technical, though, he didn't ride the wave. He took off. His feet and board were never together on the face of the wave. He just got square-pitched; never even touched the water. Just blew him apart. But see, this is what thrust Mark into his personal analogy that he was the gnarliest big-wave rider of all time. When he came in, I said to Mark, 'You were out in the water for the biggest wave I've ever seen come through.'"

"You didn't see the wave I took off on?" said Foo.

"Well. . . I saw you eat *shit*. You didn't ride anything."

That point will be debated for years. But back to Cooke, and his battle to reach the sand. "I've seen three people in my life die in the shorebreak," said Bradshaw. "With Alec, I have to admit, in a sick way, we were all up there laughing. Is this guy really gonna die? The helicopter kept coming by, but Alec was too dumb and arrogant to try and get in the basket. Finally he did start trying, and I can still see him, sticking his hand up, looking at the tube come over him. WHAM! And the basket kept coming up empty. This went on for about ten minutes. And I'm thinking, how much punishment can a person take? Finally you see these two hands emerging, underneath the basket. He grabbed his fingers in the netting. It was unreal. The Guy Who Went to Hell, man.

"Normally I don't like even talking to Alec. I really don't. But when he got in I said, 'Close one that time.' And he says, 'Naw, man, I didn't need that basket.' Just like that. I'm thinking, 'Right. *Dude*.'

"The incredible thing about that day," said Bradshaw, "is that all the people I think surf Waimea good were standing there, saying, 'I wouldn't want to be out there for anything.'"

Why does Bradshaw do this? What moves a man to go out there? "I guess it's an addiction," he says. "I have no idea, but it must be like being on drugs. Because when you're not doing it, it torments and eats away at you. When it *is* happening [long pause]... I guess it's like looking at life itself. For a moment, you've got it all. It's yours. You've gone to the very epitome of what you can do. How many people can say that in this world?

"Yes, there can be more. Is there a bigger one? Will I be in shape? Will I have the right energy level and motivation? But see, there are so few people doing it. There's nobody else to measure up to, but yourself. That's exactly it. Yourself and the next 25-foot mountain."

Even Bradshaw's father has accepted him now. "He disowned me for about two years, wouldn't talk to me, couldn't believe what I was doing. He was ashamed to tell his friends about it. It was always, 'Come on home, I'll show you the business, you can work for me.' As much as it hurt him—and it broke his heart—I couldn't do it. I'd already surfed Waimea. I realized how much more I wanted to do. There was no way I could walk away from it.

"Since he retired, in '77, my surfing has grown. When I won the Duke contest in '83, he saw it on ABC. Since then it's been 'My son, the surfing champion,' and everything's fine. They've got all sorts of memorabilia at the house."

Kenny goes back to Texas sometimes, to see the family and promote his business, but he won't ever be going back to stay. "I plan to be like [60-year-old] Peter Cole—actually surfing even more than Peter because he's got a job outside surfing. My life *is* surfing. I bought a house at the end of Ke Nui Road, so I can keep an eye on Sunset forever. I mean, until Ken Bradshaw expires, this is where he's gonna live."

The last time I saw Bradshaw, I was out on a pleasant, 6-8-foot day at Sunset. In the middle of what looked like a critical drop to me, Bradshaw noticed one of his friends paddling out. "Hey, Bob!" he cried out excitedly, still in mid-descent. "What are *you* doing out here?" Bradshaw was smiling and waving his hands, like some jovial barbecue host. He did everything but offer this guy the potato chips.

Trevor Sifton

Where do you go after Bradshaw? Someplace different. A tiny little house on Waimea Bay, where the big sets rattle the earth. Inside sits Trevor Sifton, his wife Kristin, and a worldly Australian, identified only as Peter. There is bright conversation in the room. Trevor's infant son frolics about, looking exceptional. This is Trevor's first interview, ever, and the way he surfs, it's about time.

There's a famous story about Bradshaw paddling through the '86 Billabong contest at Waimea, just heading straight out to sea, then veering north to surf 25-foot waves at outside Log Cabins. What's not so well known is that Trevor Sifton was already out there, alone. He'd paddled out through the shorebreak, an indescribable cauldron of churning whitewater. "That's intense," said Bradshaw. "I've got to know how he does that."

Different kind of cat, this Sifton (pronounced just how it looks, although people can't seem to get it right; Bradshaw pronounced it Sif-FON, and one magazine called him Siphon). He and Kristin are international fashion models. They travel around the globe, looking fabulous. Back home on the North Shore, though, Trevor is the absolute, stone-cold definition of "soul" surfer. He wants no attention whatsoever, and gets none. He likes surfing alone, preferably in enormous size, at sites too remote to be photographed.

"I'm so anti-ego that if I start feeling it around me, I'll go surf somewhere else, just out of spite," he says. "Someplace where the wind is just howling, like Phantoms [an outer reef], where it takes 20 minutes to paddle out, just to surf by myself. I don't care. I just like being out in the water, in the energy. I don't feel like I'm alone, actually. I'm *with* the water, and I've *got* myself. I'm my best companion."

"He's the kind of guy," said Mike Latronic, "and I know this is gonna happen...Ace Cool finally goes to Kaena Point when it's 40 feet, and the network TV cameras are there, the helicopters and everything else, and there's somebody dripping wet, saying, 'God, you guys should have seen it at low tide.' That's Trevor."

Sifton is one of the very few big-wave riders to have grown up on the North Shore. His childhood frame of reference — and this is all you need to know — was Jose Angel, often described by Greg Noll and Fred Van Dyke as the guttiest surfer of their era. Trevor spent a lot of time with the Angel family along the Log Cabins stretch of Ke Iki, and he saw some wondrous things.

Jose Angel stories are among the richest in all of surfing. Shortly after Angel's death in 1976, Billy Hamilton wrote, "There was a slow, easy rhythm to his gait, and he seemed to bob and sway as he ran, as if silently punching the air and dodging a rapid return of fire. I remember one day, looking out from his house, when the outside reefs from Pipeline to Sunset were breaking well over 20 feet, and the rip was running like the Colorado River. There was no way, in my mind, that anyone would want to mess around in that madness, until I saw him swimming out through a 12-foot shorebreak. In all that chaotic spillage and violent activity, he seemed completely at home."

Angel eventually came up the beach with his swim fins in one hand and a small, round ball in the other. It was his daughter's ball. She had lost it to the ocean. Jose offered Hamilton a beer and mentioned how Waimea might be good that night. Nothing else was said.

Jose had a passion for diving—black coral, in particular. On a hard-core expedition in '76, he was lost by the spotting boat, drifted 13 miles down-current, then swam five miles to the Molokai shore, where he was found in good condition. "There's no question that sharks were circling him, at least part of the way," said Hamilton. Just a month later, Angel headed for a special reef off Molokai, just loaded with black coral. There was a miscalculation. He went off into 360 feet of water, thinking he'd been rigged for 240. He didn't come up. The body was never found.

"I really love Jose Angel," said Sifton. "He'd go surf outer-reef Pipeline by himself. He'd surf Waimea on the day of a contest and tell the guys to fuck off. The waves don't happen that often, so fuck off. He'd tell the Black Shorts [water patrol] that. They're not gonna tell Jose Angel to get out of the water, he's been out there all his life. He was surfing Waimea when these guys were in underwear."

Trevor, now 27, has a cultured look about him. His father, an anthropologist, is English, his mother French. At one critical stage of Trevor's youth, his father had a contract to finish his Master's degree studies in India. "We were gone, on our way," Trevor recalls, "but the job fell through. We were living on Ke Iki, just as a stopover, but all of a sudden we were staying. I remember my mom saying, 'Oh, Cliff, it's just as well. It's gorgeous out here.'"

Trevor was four years old. Within two years he was learning to surf at Haleiwa—and grasping the realities of North Shore life. The massive swells of '69 destroyed the Sifton house, and the family spent the next several years at a number of spots around the islands.

"We moved to Chun's Reef when I was about 10. I lived next door to Rory Russell, Jock Sutherland, that whole gang, and they taught me how to *really* surf. I remember this guy, John Mobley, who lived in a tree house there. He owned a boat, used to travel and smuggle heroin back and forth, and

43

he lived up in this tree house with a shotgun. He'd shoot over the head of everyone at Chun's and say, 'This is my spot! Get out of here!' That made a big impression on me. Then we moved up to Marijuanas when I was 12, with Tommy Nellis and all them, and then up to Log Cabins, next to Jose and a lot of old-time shapers.

"I was a real rowdy, bad kid. Shit, I was stoned half the time; started when I was eight. They moved me around a lot. St. Louis high school, Kahuku, Waialua...I went through the drug years real early, thank God. I started changing my routine when I was about 16 and we moved up to Kawela Bay. I ended up running on the beach a lot, surfing some really remote spots between Kawela and Velzyland. Just went out by myself. The local guys had it as a fishing spot, and they'd actually shoot at people who tried to surf there. Yeah, it was wild. But I lived there and they let me surf it. That's where I really started liking big waves, by myself.

"So," said Trevor, looking at Peter the Australian, then me. "What do you want to know? One wave led to another, and... [laughter]."

"What about the modeling?" I asked.

"Well," he said, acting all effeminate. "I'm growing into my look [more laughter]."

It's an interesting contrast, though, the surfing and modeling lifestyles. "Here's the thing," he said. "Surfing is my hobby. That's it. I always think of when I was six years old, the first time I went out. The smell of the wax and the board, the feeling of whitewater going through my body. If I were to think about my surfing *any* other way, it would change my attitude. I'd rather be anti-social and on my own.

"The modeling is just fun. You're being used to show a product, and to me, that's not an ego thing. You meet a lot of people, spend all kinds of great money. I can travel anywhere and work decently, competitively. You gotta understand, there's a million guys who look like me. It's all in yourself, how well you keep yourself together. A lot of models out there are completely phony, just like phony surfers, and they don't get anywhere."

"So Kristin's a model, too?" I ask.

"She likes to think so," he says, smiling.

"She models vicariously through Trevor," says Peter.

This modeling thing tends to throw people on the North Shore. "I mean, people think he's some sort of fag," said Nellis, chuckling at the absurdity. "Hey. He's got a lot of balls, and he's an individual, and he's different. He rides *big* fucking waves. And nobody's givin' him any kind of shit, either. I remember that day he and Bradshaw surfed outer Rockpiles [Log Cabins]. I saw him paddle out from the beach. I knew exactly who it was out there. I didn't know it was Bradshaw, but I knew it was Trevor."

"I looked at Ken totally different that day," said Sifton. "I said wow, Ken, you paddled down. That's different of you. That's neat. I mean, nobody's really joining me out there. I'm not really *asking* them."

Imagine this: You paddle out through terrifying shore-break, alone. Twenty minutes later, you're a half-mile out in waves pushing 25 feet. You lose your board. You swim *in* through the shorebreak. You grab your board and head back out. Trevor Sifton did that, twice, on the day he met Bradshaw at outer Rockpiles. He does that because it wouldn't occur to him to surf another way.

"For guys like Ricky Grigg and Peter Cole, that stuff is just routine," he says. "We don't have that morale any more on the North Shore. I would like to think I'm the old style. Primitive. Single fin. Cords, no way. And with Kenny, we're like little kids out there. Like [excitedly], 'Trevor, where do you place yourself?' Or, 'What do you do now?' It's fun to be out with someone like that. I'm the same way. Man, the energy level out there...you just can't imagine it."

Shortly after Bradshaw arrived that day, Trevor broke the ice. "My first wave was fantastic. Ken was on the shoulder, and I was screaming and howling. The second wave, we took off together. He pulled out halfway, I rode it a little farther and bounced off. The chop was way too big. Then we got caught inside, real bad. His board just snapped in half. I guess Kenny didn't really get a wave, but it was new to him, and he's cautious, and I understand that. He has the *desire* to be out there, and I know that, and I like that." At this moment, Sifton sounded a lot like Bradshaw: the same soft, high-pitched voice, the same inflections.

How about the other characters in the North Shore theater? "When it's really big, you'll see Clyde [Aikau] at Waimea. This guy doesn't even train; he just comes out and pummels the place. Takes off on 30-foot waves and just blows people *away*. Owl will be really crazed, smoke a big joint and do it. Gary Speece—takes off on giant stuff. Darrick's really into it. Roger Erickson. I'd say I'm a little on the crazed side, while Ken is conservative. Not in a bad sense, a hesitant or over-cautious sense, but he's more into precision and all that. It's interesting, he's really intense and boastful, but he's very calculating. He likes to know exactly where he is out there, how often the sets are coming, and at what size. That's the kind of surfer I'd like to be as I get older.

"The ego of surfing Waimea Bay...it's like the Roman Colosseum," he says. "I'll admit I've got an ego, as well. I end up using it to intimidate people out in the water, to jockey myself into position. But those egos have to jibe. Some people are completely into their own routine and just eliminate everyone else out there. With Mark Foo, you can *feel* his ego, just for himself. He doesn't really acknowledge or compliment people out there. And that's fine. That's Mark, and he's a hell of a surfer.

"But you should see, for example, Pipeline when it gets big. I paddled down there once on a 10-foot day, just to check out the scene. Everybody's out: Dane, Derek Ho, Johnny Boy, Ronnie Burns, Tony Moniz. All the local boys. All the guys who surf it good at that size. And there's only three, four waves a set. So who gets all the waves? Of *course*, those guys. But

they'll be yelling each other on. 'Go, Ronnie, yeah, yeah!'
They're supporting each other.

"I'm not gonna say Mark Foo is a jerk, because he's never
been a jerk to me. I've been a jerk to *him* [laughs]. But I don't
want to have that around me. You're sitting *this* close to some
guy with an 11-foot board in 30-foot waves. You've gotta *dis-cuss* this. If I don't see that, I'll just go somewhere else. I
choose not to squabble."

There was one particular day at outer Rockpiles—just a
week after the Bradshaw excursion—when Trevor didn't think
he'd be coming back. Caught inside a 30-foot set, alone, he
found himself panicking after going over the first monstrous
ledge. "I wanted to get the hell out of there. I was on a James
Jones 9-4, and they're thick, but real narrow. All I remember is
paddling straight up the wave like this [vertical], and I made it
over the top...but the wind blew me back. I turned around
and saw Turtle Bay, Beach Park, the whole coastline, and as I
was going down backwards, I just told myself, get a *big* breath.
It was just a free-fall.

"I went down effortlessly. I went down deep. I didn't feel
the pressure of how far down I was until the wave pulled me
around and took me *back* down to the bottom again. I got up
fairly quick—my board was still with me—and my main con-cern was the next wave. You need to know how many waves
come in a set, and how often they come. You *have* to know
that. But in the middle of the ocean, you're talking about sea
swells. It's tough to get a handle on that. You can drift 100
yards off the peak without even knowing it.

"I saw the third wave and it was clean, no whitewash on it,
so I knew it was even bigger. When it broke, it displaced water
about 20 feet in front of me. I mean, 50 yards moved, just
parted for this lip. I didn't have much breath; my heart was
beating fast. I knew from Jose not to dive too deep. It takes
too much energy to go way down, and if the wave starts
rolling you, hey, you can't hold your breath for longer than a
minute."

Trevor didn't think he could, anyway. On this wave, the worst nightmare of his life, he reckons he was down there 90 seconds. "Beyond my limit. All I remember was black, all around me, no air, and the pressure in my ears was excruciating. My arms were going for air pockets, but I wasn't getting anywhere. At that point, after about 20 strokes, I told myself that I was going to die. Can't last any longer. And right at the point where I decided, 'Trevor, this is it,' time stopped. Everything about my life went shooting through my head. And suddenly something told me, 'Trevor, you're not going to die.' I felt a release in the pressure. I popped up. I was choking, and my board was 200 yards in, and my mind just went blank."

There's really nothing in sports to compare with this. In auto racing, the accidents happen all too fast. If you get your neck snapped by a linebacker, you probably never saw him coming. But in surfing, coming to terms with death—or at least the possibility—is an ongoing crisis in big waves. The set is building outside, and it's so *beautiful,* aesthetically. People are watching in awe from the beach: the blue water, the stiff offshore winds, the 40-foot walls charging in from the open ocean. If you're out there with nothing but your body, your wits and a surfboard, that set can be your coffin. The massive first wave, the even *bigger* second wave. More of them outside. You can't panic; that takes *all* your breath away. But if it's the biggest set you've ever seen, how do you stay calm? At *any* level of the sport?

"I think suffocating is the worst kind of death," says Sifton. "Being drowned. You lose your air, you have time to think about it, and then you have that point where you have to tell yourself, I give up. That's what separates surfing from everything."

Sometimes, the experience is just too severe. Kimo Hollinger was never the same after his near-drowning at Waimea. Greg Noll took off on a 30-foot wave (minimum, they say) at Makaha in '69, survived it, and found himself unable to surf seriously thereafter, finally giving up the sport

48

entirely. Dozens of North Shore surfers have taken on their biggest challenge and *not* come back.

"You have to want it, and spend energy thinking about it, when it's *not* big," says Sifton. "When I started surfing big waves, they all thought I was crazy, like I was on a mission. And I *was* on a mission. I still am. I love the pure energy of the ocean and the sun, and I enjoy the craziness of it. I love speeding, I love height. I like jumping 60 feet off a cliff into water. I like that a *lot*. That's what makes me go for it.

"The fear? It's not fear, it's adrenalin. Hey, going over the falls? I *love* that. I don't give a shit. My friends tease me about it: 'Let's go out and watch Trevor go over the falls.' And hey, you've got to know how to do that, and do it right. All that wiping out helps you get used to the fun."

I had never seen Trevor Sifton in the water, which made good enough sense, because I'm not too keen on 50-foot drops where you can barely see land. Amazingly, on the very morning after our interview, we were both out at Gas Chambers. It was glassy, clean, mostly unmakeable and a consistent 6-8 feet—all I care to handle. And there was Trevor, and Peter, and another friend, just having a ridiculously good time. Basically, they were watching Trevor go over the falls. He'd take off time after time, put himself in a horrible situation, and just get annihilated. Thundering laughter, all around. Finally Trevor's board gave in; simply broke in two. And suddenly they were all gone, undoubtedly chuckling on their way to some other place. It was the damndest thing.

Off The Wall

A gallery of North Shore quotations, accumulated from various sources over the years:

"Every year it is different. Every year it is the same."
— Drew Kampion

"When I'm in Hawaii, it's not my favorite surf in the world. But when I'm *not* there, it is."
— Michael Tomson

"I lived in New York until I was 9. I used to like hot dawgs, goin' to the pahk. I got rid of it in California. Over there you'd better be ready to say, 'Dude...cosmic.'"
— Mike Latronic

"Surfers have incredible egos, and they always think they're right. They don't hang out in groups, they're usually a little bit different than everyone else in their family, they can't drive cars worth shit, stuff like that."
— Tom Nellis

"East Coast guys are the worst. They're calling 'double overhead' on a 5-foot wave. I tell 'em if that's the case, I rode an 80-foot wave at Waimea."
— Randy Rarick

"I can sit there all day and stare at Pipeline. Just stare out at the surf."

— Gerry Lopez

"Jackie Dunn. Son of a gun."

— Rory Russell

"The big-wave riders of the past would have preferred to drown, rather than rely on someone else to pull them through a situation beyond their capabilities."

— Fred Van Dyke

"If you can't have a spectacular maneuver, have a spectacular wipeout. It's good for the public."

— Martin Potter

"Shhh…don't tell anyone I like Thrusters."

— Darrick Doerner

"All this hype about triathletes and stuff…not one of those guys would last five minutes at Sunset."

— Mark Foo

"No one could beat Jeff Hakman."

— Jonathan Paarman

"After surfers, the No. 2 group to be injured or die is the military. Those guys are famous for coming down here a little bit drunk from the night before. And you don't get too far wearin' Levis."

— Bernie Baker

"I'm surprised I'm still living. Yeah, I'm a dead man, 30 times over."

— Owl Chapman

"One 25-footer is better than a hundred 18-footers, so why bother with them?"

— Peter Cole

"The true sense means casting aside all the bullshit and paddling out there on your own board, paddling into the wave under your own steam, riding the damn thing, and then getting out of there on your own."

— Greg Noll

"I learned to accept myself for what I was: not good or bad, not a hero or a coward—just a surfer. I figured that was good enough for me."

—Dorian Paskowitz

Mark Foo

Mark Foo was driving up one of the back roads toward Wahiawa one rainy night when his car skidded, spun out, careened off a telephone pole and plunged over the side, landing upside down some 40 feet below. "As the whole thing unfolded, everything was clear to me, like it was happening in slow motion. I was cognitive, calculating, aware of what I had to do. I wanted to get into the passenger seat, but my seat belt had jammed from the earlier impact. So I had to crush myself down [rolls himself into a ball] and put my arm up where the roof was going to come down. I put myself where I thought would be the safest—and I made it out of there."

Foo told that story because it reminded him of January '85, the day he encountered that unspeakably large wave with James Jones and Alec Cooke at Waimea Bay. The experience felt the same to him: a life-threatening crisis, but something he could handle with the proper thought, energy and reaction. Without question, there is an aura around Mark Foo. He's like Bradshaw that way, and Jones and Roger Erickson and those other 10-15 men who truly challenge the Bay. You have no idea what they've experienced out there, but they seem to bring little pieces of it back with them. At times, it fairly radiates off their bodies.

At 32, Foo wears the proof of his North Shore commitment. There's a large, nasty scar behind his left shoulder, the result of a Haleiwa surfing accident, and another one along the outside of his left ankle. He broke his fibula bone, a complete dislocation of the ankle, trying to pull off a floater on a small day at Pipeline in February of '89. Doctors told him he'd be out of the water 10 months after that injury, but Mark didn't quite see it that way. He was surfing the North Shore again in 10 *weeks*. "While I was in the cast, I helped it along with mental healing, focusing on actually seeing the bones grow and join," he said. "I also experimented with herbal remedies and acupuncture. I just visualized myself surfing again." And so he did. The man has a knack for getting things done.

Born in Singapore, raised in Honolulu, Foo grew up surfing alongside the likes of Dane Kealoha, Bobby Owens, Buttons Kaluhiokalani and Mark Liddell—although he hardly compared with them. He was just a skinny kid with no athletic presence at all. "I didn't even learn to swim until I was 10 years old," he says. "I was scared of the water, and my family was *very* anti-surfing. First-generation Chinese. I'm a little bit *haole*, but my upbringing is definitely Chinese values. You went to school, you became a doctor or engineer.

"I sort of lost my parents for a long time. I left home when I was 14, because I wanted to surf. It's OK now, but nothing would make them happier than if I quit surfing and went back to school. Even now."

In those early days on the South Shore, "I surfed the whitewater for a year, which was really a long time. They used to call me the Whitewater King. I was, like, 12. Once a week, on Sundays, I'd get to go to Waikiki and surf the green waves [laughter]."

That seemed like the ultimate, but something was happening inside him. "Now that I look back, I believe it was something I was born to do. I moved up from Waikiki to Ala Moana, then Kaiser's, then out to the North Shore—Chun's, Velzyland, Haleiwa. Eventually I moved into the lineup at Sunset. I really felt I was living my destiny; this is what I was put here for. A lot of guys had more ability, more talent, and they grew up right here. But you look at the guys who pioneered big-wave surfing. They all came from somewhere else. Even the guys in the mid-'70s. Somehow, the Hawaiian guys would stop somewhere along the line. Like Buttons—he could do *anything* he wanted on a wave, but he wouldn't do it over 8 feet. Why those guys stopped and I didn't, I don't know. That desire, I guess, is something you're born with."

I mentioned Michael Holton. Back in '74, the first and last winter I attempted to surf big Pipeline, I saw a 14-year-old kid absolutely shredding the place, attacking massive drops with an incredible sort of reckless calm. To this day, it's one of the most amazing things I've ever seen. "I used to be in awe of him," said Foo. "He went out and charged. Not at Sunset, though. He didn't keep going. He had the ability and the guts at that age, but his progress just stopped. Oh, he was awesome back then. The only guy in his league would have been Michael Ho. I mean, when he was a *baby*, Michael Ho was incredible [laughter].

"Holton's still surfing. There's even a spot [along the Laniakea stretch] named after his family. But it's funny…it's always the guys who came here from somewhere else. Erickson, Doerner, Bradshaw, myself…."

Trevor Sifton is obviously an exception, but if you ask Foo how many North Shore kids went on to be consistent big-wave riders, he answers, "None. Eddie [Aikau] went to Roosevelt High, like me. You've got Mike Latronic and Brock Little, but they moved here from California. A lot of guys are dead, too. It's a surfing community. Therefore it's a drug community, pretty much. It's just too hard to survive growing up out here. Too much drugs. You get burned out.

"I used to smoke it when I was a little kid in elementary school," he said. "It got too strong [laughter]. I can't do it, anyway. I'm confused enough as it is."

"Misunderstood" might be the better word. There seems to be a real indifference toward Foo on the North Shore these days, and not just from Bradshaw. He's sort of like that kid in high school who does everything right, gets straight A's, and sails off into stardom. The regular kids just hate that sort of thing.

But then again, Mark gives them plenty of ammunition. He's a self-described loner who neither seeks nor desires friendships with other surfers ("I guess I don't have many friends," he says, not at all bothered by the admission). He has no problem promoting himself, through articles or photographs. He writes a surf column, appears regularly on surf-related television shows, and usually handles the on-the-beach TV interviews during the major Hawaiian contests (nothing to be scoffed at; most surfers are repulsed by the idea of being interviewed so soon after they've left the water, but Foo usually gets his man).

"I came up as the new guy, on the outside," he says. "Nobody else progressed into big-wave riding from my generation. On the tour, there's always some new, 16-year-old phenomenon, and the guys get used to it. For big-wave riders, it's something unusual. They don't appreciate someone stealing their thunder.

"As far as making money...I was very disillusioned when I began surfing seriously. I felt what we were doing in big waves, as athletes, just shit on those guys walking on golf greens, or hitting fuzzy balls over a net. I was tired of being called a surf bum—by society, even by my own mother. People I really admired were being called that. Surfing is a pretty big deal in Australia and Japan, and here's Hawaii, where we've given the sport to the world, and we're the *most* behind! Less money, less sponsorship, less prestige. I sat at home one day and decided to do something about it. I started doing radio, television, writing, whatever I could do to educate the public.

"I really felt this was part of my destiny, too. It seemed that Dane, Bobby and the other guys in my generation didn't have the talent or the interest to be a voice for Hawaiian surfing. Somebody had to do it, so I guess it was me. I certainly haven't been out to promote just myself. I think I've been fair to everybody, whether I like them personally or not. I've probably promoted Ken Bradshaw more than anyone in the world. I've just tried to educate people about the virtues of surfing, because I think we are very lucky people. We know what makes us happy, we know how to pursue it, and that's really one of the secrets of life. The majority of people never discover that. In my mind, surfers have it over everybody else. That's what I'm trying to promote."

The North Shore wave-measuring system really amuses Foo. "It's such a joke, these guys. They're calling it 18 feet, and if you want to be honest, we're talking about 40-foot faces, even 50, 60. You're paddling out, you see a guy on a wave, and it's 10, 12 times as big as he is! But, no. It's an unwritten law. You're really pushing it if you call it 20 feet. I called a wave 20 feet in front of George Downing one time, and he laughed at me."

The old school seems to be jumping Foo at every turn, particularly when it comes to equipment and surfing the outer reefs. "I use leashes. I don't have all this reverence that some of these guys have. Actually, I have profound respect for what the older guys did — Ricky Grigg, Buzzy Trent, Jose Angel, Greg Noll, and of course Eddie Aikau. They did it without leashes. Those guys were extraordinary; they didn't know the bottom or the lineups. What they did took balls. But I want to surf those same waves with the approach I take to small-wave surfing. So I take the same type of equipment out there.

"I went out to Waimea with a three-fin, because it just wasn't *ingrained* in me to go charging out there on a single-fin without a leash. I took what I'd been using at Sunset, as good as it got. And it wasn't even a conventional three-fin, it was the back-fin 'boomerang' design they use in windsurfing. I mean, single-fins had been obsolete at every place but Waimea since the early '80s, but nobody had the nerve to experiment in 20-foot Waimea surf. So I think I opened up the performance level out there. That's the contribution I made. Not that those other guys were copying me, but it took somebody to go out there and prove it could be done. Now a lot of people use them, Bradshaw included.

"Kenny and I are just very different. Size. Race. Values. He resents me a lot. He had like a domain, his little thing, and I guess I copped some of it. But I think I've been good for him; I've kept him motivated. The rivalry we've had has pushed the sport ahead. I don't know if I've ever said, 'I'm the best at the Bay,' but I honestly feel that nobody surfs it any better. Every time I come in, I feel the same way. And I think that's good for surfing.

"I've always likened it to the martial arts, where you couldn't become accepted, couldn't really take off, unless you had personality. Boxing, too—not fighters, but personalities. A Muhammad Ali, a Bruce Lee, people can relate to those guys. When you think about it, most of the big-wave riders were these big, bearded, macho-looking guys. Nobody could really relate to people like Bradshaw and Roger Erickson, especially little kids growing up in Hawaii. But here's Mark Foo, a smaller guy who had made his name in small-wave surfing. I wasn't some super-athlete, I was a guy they'd surfed with at Chun's Reef for 10 years. Now some young surfer can say, 'If he can do it, so can I.' And that gives the sport a personality injection."

And the business of using boats, helicopters, and the like to get ahead? "That stuff, 'If you can't paddle in and out, don't go,' that's a crock. You want to *ride* the waves. That's the name of the game. I want my energy to surf, not paddle out and swim in. That's what my energy is for. It's not this macho trip, 'I'm such a water man, I can get out and back on my own.' To me, it's about surfing. If I lose my board, hey—I swim in. But I want to use my energy the best way. That's what progress is for, to advance with it.

"I mean, Kenny says he's going to paddle out from Waimea, out a mile, then down the beach three miles, then go surf. That's ridiculous. You couldn't be at your peak. I don't think he enjoyed paddling through the surf that day. He was probably pissed off, because we were surfing the contest in perfect Waimea, two or three guys out, and being paid, and he'd been knocked out of it earlier. Actually [smiling], he was *very* pissed off. That was a *dream*, what we had out there."

Foo first surfed Waimea in 1977. He remembers taking horrendous gas on his first wave when Shaun Tomson dropped in on him, and feeling pretty frustrated about it. "As I look back on it, though, it was cool," Foo says. "It was just another confirmation that big-wave surfing was my calling, that I was meant to do it. Shaun Tomson was the world champion, with a lot of good years ahead of him, and I was a kid, but I was taking off deeper than he was—on my first wave there."

Foo has lived at Waimea for years, and his surfing routine has been crafted down to a science. "I study the place from home, a little deck I've got upstairs, where I can see the waves. If I head down there, I'm going out. I always take my boards from the same place, go down to the break the same way. I give myself a speech, a meditative sort of thing, and I stretch —always the same. I want my body to be centered, my breathing to be relaxed. Free-flowing concentration, I call it. You're concentrating, but you're not trying to. That makes it normal for me. And I never go surfing *with* someone at Waimea. I kind of stay in the bushes in a corner. Nobody even sees me, I don't think. And if they do, I don't care. I feel at ease, in my element.

"When you paddle out there, you look at guys' faces, into their eyes, and you can tell who really loves it. It's just a select few that have that look, and the discipline to stay put when it really gets heavy. I mean, the horizon just blacks out. You'll see the outer reefs go off outside Logs or Alligators, and it just goes black. It's coming. And you know exactly where. Guys are running and hiding, scrambling all around. If you really want it, you just stay right on that boil.

"There's a whole generation of red-hot kids, world champions, Top Sixteen guys, but they're terrified. Brock Little [just 23] is the *one* guy in his generation that was born with it. This is what he wants to do. Roger [Erickson] has the look. Darrick Doerner, too; he surfs it progressively and he's really underrated. James [Jones] is really good at 15 to 18 feet. After 20 feet, if it's closing out or on the fringe, he doesn't like it. But he was a big inspiration to me. For a long time, he was the only guy I saw get in the tube out there. But he has his limit."

"Do you?" I asked him.

"I haven't found it yet."

Guess not. If you (a) go under the all-time killer wave, (b) turn around and ride a 30-footer, as Mark Foo did in 1985, and (c) keep going back for more, you're in a pretty private little world.

"For me, the more adverse the situation, the more peaceful I am," he says. "That's when I become truly centered. It's really funny. Basically I'm kind of high-strung and nervous. I'm scared of speed, I'm scared of heights, I don't gamble. I'm not really into athletics. Surfing big waves is the combination of all these things that are against my nature. That's why I feel there's a bigger purpose to it."

Foo had been sick for 10 days, just out of commission, when that big day arrived. He was driving to the Haleiwa post office when he noticed Waimea breaking—with nobody out. "I just ran down there and paddled right out," he said. Bradshaw had just come in from his 45-minute swim; Jones and Cooke were heading out.

"I caught four or five waves real quick, but it was real ledgy and west that day. The water was just…heavy, somehow. Just these huge barrels, and they looked like steel. They didn't look like water, they looked like steel. Guys were looking uncomfortable. Kenny [on the beach] *really* did, and that threw me off. So I was the last one to see the set come."

Even the old-timers, the Nolls and the Currens and the Trents, would have bowed to this wave. It was beyond reality, totally without precedent. "I actually kind of laughed," Foo recalled. "It was like a cartoon, almost. Just so ridiculous. Here I had just seen 30-foot waves that were inside out, like holes in the ocean, you know? Those were the biggest waves I'd ever *seen.* Then I turn and look...and *this* thing is like twice as big!"

So here was Mark Foo, four years after the fact, discussing the North Shore wave for the ages, and suddenly he was back at the scene. His mind was racing, trying to recall every little detail. His dialogue went into fast-forward mode, making no sense at all:

"These guys were...and I...and this is why I feel like... OK, so I was on the in...and what I did, so I paddled right... and the thing is..."

That's OK, Mark. You can talk about it any old way.

"The thing is, it turned into a *left,*" he said, still blown away by the notion. "Waimea had turned into a left. It was a new break. I paddled for the channel, but I paddled right into the peak. The worst place. I had the worst of the impact. For some reason, I didn't lose my board, and everyone else did. [J.P. Patterson, a big-wave bodyboarder of grim resolve, was also caught inside.] And I mean, for me to be out there, that was fate. For me to keep my board, while the other guys lost theirs ...*got* to be fate. And this was a monster board; it would snap your leash in a second.

"The wave broke top to bottom, and luckily, I was in an envelope. I was right in that envelope under the big explosion. It wasn't the worst hold-down I've ever had, but I'll tell you, my board and I were just insignificant. There was no climbing the leash, getting pulled by the board, any of that. Insignificant.

"OK, so now Waimea's a left. So OK, I'm gonna catch one of these lefts and head for the corner. About four or five more close-out sets came, and I was just dodging 'em. The helicopter was trying to get me to come in—after they'd pulled James and Alec out—but I had my board. I was comfortable. I didn't feel like I needed it. I could surf in."

Which he did, and if the general consensus was 30 feet, it had to be one of the biggest waves ever ridden. Sorry, attempted. Just what *did* happen, anyway?

"Nobody could have made that wave," he said. "I know what's rideable, and what isn't. It was the unridden realm. I was in early. I was standing. I was low. It was a technically perfect takeoff. But the thing was too concave; they *all* are at that size. I fell in the air, maybe 20-30 feet. I've had takeoffs where you're completely released, and if you land properly, you're all right. But I was going so fast, I didn't even penetrate the water when I landed. And then the lip just lands *right* on your head . . . [laughing] it's pretty punishing."

Now he was down deep, way down in the Waimea washing machine, "and when it's really heavy like that, seeing stars is only the first thing," he said. "You get brown, then it goes gray, and after that, it's just black. But you can't let go of your consciousness. Trying to 'relax' out there, that's a crock of shit. You're *fighting*. You're at the bottom, you're out of air, it's a *struggle* to get back up. If you just 'go with it,' you won't come back. I fought, hard as I could. And I made it back up."

Pretty soon, the interview was over. Foo had been eyeing Sunset out the window of my rented house, and now he was heading out there. Eddie Erickson, a surfing friend from Malibu, had been listening to Foo's stories with me. We were both sort of stunned.

"Tell you what," Eddie said later. "If I went through something like that, I'd want to be recognized. Couple photos wouldn't hurt, either."

Pipeline at its most pristine ...

...And its most horrifying.

Rob Gilley, Surfer Magazine

The North Shore in essence

Craig Fineman, Surfer Magazine

Dane Kealoha, the unrivaled master of Backdoor

Craig Fineman

Johnny Boy Gomes, Pipeline. On any given day, the hottest surfer in Hawaii

Jose Angel (above, at Sunset), a legend among Hawaiian water men

There aren't many backsiders among today's Waimea crew. Angel did it regularly.

Trevor Sifton on a modeling job (above) and at Waimea Bay (right), free-falling to the bottom behind Bill Sickler. "I remember that wave," Trevor says. "That was fun."

Sequence by Gordinho, Surfer Magazine

Gordinho

Trevor's surf photo collection consists of about 15 slides. This one sums it up well.

Titus Kinimaka, his leg badly broken, helped out of the water at Waimea Bay by (left to right) Vince Klyn, Ken Bradshaw and Darrick Doerner. It was Christmas Day.

Fearless Greg Noll, taking a horrible wipeout at Waimea in the late '50s

Tom Nellis has been a dedicated, low-key Waimea rider for nearly 20 years. If it's big, he's out there.

Nellis' surfing partner, Tony Roy, at massive Pipeline. Says Tom: "The more I look at this wave, the heavier it gets. Tony was probably smiling the whole time."

Tom Nellis, streaking through inside Pipeline. It was 15 feet on takeoff.

Tom Nellis

Out in "the country," as the North Shore is called, things aren't always so country. Fast-food chains are starting to creep their way in, a second large hotel will be going up on the northern end, and there are few secret spots left. Just when you think you're onto something, here come 16 guys in flaming rainbow vests, with about six hundred too many decals littering their boards.

That's why it's refreshing to find surfers like Tom Nellis, because they keep the "country" alive. When I mentioned Nellis' name to Darrick Doerner, he smiled and said, "Good dude. Fifteen, 20 years later, he's still here. All-around water man, all-around beer drinker. You know, still alive and kickin'. Settin' a good example. [Southern accent] Hell, yeah."

My lasting impression of Nellis is this bearded, burly guy on a bicycle, heading down to Waimea Bay with nothing but a pair of trunks and a surfboard. He definitely has a backwoods feel, right down to the high-pitched cackle in his voice. Actually, Tom and his French-Canadian wife Diane are quite civil company, doing splendidly in a nice house at a choice location. They're about as decent and down-to-earth as you'll find. But it's like the man said: get Tom together with some hard-core surfers and a few beers, and you've got old-style North Shore. Pure talent, no nonsense, and what Tom likes to call "sack." That would be "guts," to you city folk.

It's kind of amazing that Tom's still surfing, to be honest. He's developed a badly displaced pelvis over the last two years, the result of constant pressure from his hamstrings, and there are times when he can hardly walk. "The thing just shifted on me," he says. That can be a lifetime's worth of pain, but Nellis refuses to accept the notion that he's wounded. "I don't want anybody cuttin' on me. If I have to wear pink panties around the North Shore for a week to get well, I'll do it. If some jerk comes down the street with a bottle and some snake oil, I'll buy 'em both. I'll get a whole bunch of opinions before I get an operation."

While most people would be shuffling around in self-pity, Tom saw no problem taking his board and his back out to 15-foot Makaha recently. It went pretty well, too, until someone dropped in on him, right as Nellis was entering the legendary bowl. "I made the ultimate mistake," he said. "Instead of jumping off, I straightened out and tried to hold onto my board. Now, the whitewater at Makaha is something to behold. It's *really* tall. I never let go, just got spun around a hundred times. Really torqued my back up bad. I don't know, I just can't re-educate myself to step off my board like that."

At 35, Nellis isn't any kind of "name" on the North Shore, but he is known. He actually invented some out-of-the-way breaks in the '70s, and if you hang around those places, you'll see a distinctive type of surfer: a little older, probably hung over, riding a Nellis board (he shapes for Lightning Bolt on Maui) and surfing with classic Hawaiian style and power. These guys really take issue with the modern, slash-it-up, embarrass-the-wave movement. I mean, they'll actually suggest you leave the water if you're not surfing the place right.

"Just guys who know how to live," says Tom.

Nellis is known around Waimea Bay, too, and well he should be. He basically lives for big surf on the North Shore, and while he's been a bit out of commission lately, he's surfed 20-foot Waimea about as much as anyone over the years. He'll be back out there, too. There's no other way of looking at it.

"To me, he's like a Bill Sickler," says Ken Bradshaw. "There's a whole group of guys who came here because it was Hawaii, but Tom didn't come to be a famous surfer. He came here to live and surf. I respect a guy like that."

Mark Foo has described Nellis as a "Waimean," and he still can't get over the time Tom broke his board almost immediately on one of the Bay's better days. "Tom simply went home and built a new board," says Foo. "He was riding waves on it by lunchtime." Nellis confirms this, modestly: "Took me about five hours. The fin rope was still goin' off when I hit the water. That was 3-4 years ago, a 9-6 board. I'm still riding it."

"He's just one of those guys who come out of the woodwork," said Foo. "That's the underground, the old school. They have a sixth sense, I think. You never see these guys, and then Waimea starts to break and they're *there.*"

Tony Roy is one of those guys. As far as Nellis can tell, only two committed North Shore surfers have ever come out of Poway High School, about a 60-mile drive inland from San Diego. Those two are Nellis and Roy, classmates in 1970. And these guys are *beyond* serious. They've ridden Pipeline together when it was breaking past the second reef. They've taken on maxed-out spots all over the North Shore, places that can barely be seen when they're going off. I remember one morning Tom and Tony stopped by my rented house near Haleiwa, wondering if I'd join them in the water. That was a moment of stark terror, wondering where *these* guys might go, but it was a clean, 8-foot day at a spot that was only moderately terrifying. What a break.

I had a solid memory of Tony Roy from 1976, when the historic assault by Shaun Tomson, Rabbit Bartholomew, Mark Richards, etc., was in full rage. I made a journal entry on January 27 of that year, noting that filmmaker Bill Delaney was shooting priceless 12-foot waves at Pipeline (it became the closing sequence of his film, *Free Ride*). But it wasn't Shaun or Rabbit that I remembered most. It was Tony Roy, breaking the ice around 7:30 that morning. He went out there alone and took three waves, riding with the casual arrogance of a punk hanging out on street corner. He made two of those waves, got obliterated on the third, then came in. Suddenly it was OK for everyone else to go out.

"He's just always been a maniac," says Nellis. "We used to hitch-hike from Poway to go surfing. He finally got a car, but he never could drive. He got maybe 3-4 cars and crashed every one of 'em. Not drunk, he was just too hyper. We used to take this dirt road, an old stagecoach route from San Diego County to the Del Mar racetrack. It's probably paved by now. We'd just go fast and crash [laughs]. He still can't drive."

Nellis remembers being "a little shrimp" in those days, but he came from a tough family. One of his six brothers, Marty, was a three-time All-America wrestler in college, and Tom combined wrestling with football (linebacker) in high school before setting his sights on Hawaii. Unlike so many others, Tom didn't take much abuse from his parents when he chose the surfing lifestyle —but then again, his father wasn't a normal sort of guy. "Pretty incredible" is how Tom describes him.

Donald Nellis was a Golden Gloves boxing champion of Chicago at the age of 16. He was a captain in the Navy, serving five terms in Viet Nam and heading up the special-forces group known as the Seals. He taught underwater demolition, traveled extensively, and told stories of a wave breaking completely over the bridge of his cruiser ship in the South China Sea. Tom was born in Panama, because Donald was head of naval operations in the Panama Canal at the time. "He's a character, and a real dedicated family guy," says Tom. "He always had the feeling, do whatever you want to do in life. Don't let anybody say you can't. Just be sure you do it well. I remember when I left for Hawaii after my junior year, he said, 'Why go to Hawaii when you could go to Malaysia and Indonesia? That's where all the surf is. Hawaii's too crowded.' Turns out he had been at Pipeline in the 1950s with some of the guys from his underwater demolition team. I showed him the place once and he said, 'Oh, yeah, we used to come down here and bodysurf. My friend used to own that house over there. Guess I should have bought the damn thing.'"

That would have been nice, but when Tom got to the North Shore in the summer of '71, he didn't much care about luxury. He took a room at a friend's house across the street from Marijuanas reef and met Tom Eberly, a noted shaper who lived in the area. "Eberly and his wife really went out of their way for me," he said. "He treated me like a younger brother. Tom taught me a lot about self-respect, and respect in general. He was a class guy and a great surfer, and he used to kid me a lot, like, 'Too bad you're going back in the fall. There's no surf here now. And even if you *did* stay, you'd never get a job. You'll just go back to California, because you're afraid the waves are gonna get big.'

"So I put him on the spot," said Nellis. "I said, 'Why don't *you* give me a job? I can sand boards as good as you. I'm not *completely* retarded.' So I shaped a couple boards, fixed some dings, and enrolled myself in school [Waialua High]. They let me stay on at the house, and from that time on, I've just surfed and worked. That's it. That's all I've been doing ever since."

The surf came up, all right, and Nellis found that when it came to surfing the North Shore, he was never short on "sack." One of his first sessions was at cranking, 10-12-foot Laniakea. The first time he saw Waimea break, he was out there. He fell in with a local crew of surfers including Walter Woods, Jeff Peterson and Dean Michioka, all of them between 16 and 18 years old. "Those guys had the idea that if you didn't surf Waimea, you didn't surf," says Nellis. "And I mean, no shit. They were into it. It was good for me to be in a crowd like that. They weren't into dope, they were just goofy kids, no weird ego trips, and they all worked."

Nellis remembers a lot of superb Waimea riders from those days—Reno Abellira, Rick Irons, Mike Taylor, the Aikaus, "and the *phenomenal* Mike Miller," he said. "Nobody could ever touch him. Big, lanky guy. He had a feel for the place, a real good rhythm for it, and a lotta sack. He took more really big waves than anyone."

Although he got very little credit for it, Nellis did some radical backside surfing at second-reef Pipeline in the late '70s and early '80s. "It gets a little nasty after 10 feet, but if you do catch a good wave out there, it's an incredible experience," he says. "There's nothin' like Pipeline. Nowhere. I remember Tony took me out on a big day once, and you'd think he'd have a big advantage over me, goin' frontside. But Pipeline is ideal for backside—it really is. You never spin out on a good wave because it's so hollow; it's smooth and glassy because it stands up so straight. Frontside you can get locked in better, but you really don't have much advantage as to making the wave. And as it gets bigger, it gets taller but less critical. So we're sitting *way* the hell out there—like, in front of Off the Wall, and three times farther out than inside Pipeline. And this guy [Roy]...he just keeps paddling out. I'm thinking, what *is* this? He's like 50-60 yards outside of me. So I take this wave through the second reef, and it was just a smoker, pushing 20 feet, and I took it all the way through to the sandbar. Now I'm paddling back out, and I see this guy take off *way* out there. And of course it was Tony, 'cause me and him were the only ones out. It wasn't that perfect a day, but I let him talk me into it [laughs].

"So he's just riding this thing—through the sandbar, all the way to Beach Park, right up to the sand. He just stepped off his board and waited for me to come in. I never got another wave. I got caught inside, barely even *made* it in. And that was the only wave that came in like that all day. It just gravitated to Tony, and he took it. And I mean, you don't even attempt to ride that wave. It was just one of those giant piles of shit. But he whipped around, took it, and stepped off his board on the beach. Pissed me off."

Nellis' stoke for Pipeline took a severe blow in '84, on a solid 12-foot day. He talked a friend into surfing the place one afternoon, "and even at that size, they were breaking on that inside reef, which is really strange for Pipeline. These things were just cement mixers. I took off on this...just *perfect* wave. Like I said, backside—no problem. I was in the tube, *gone*, but I knew I was comin' out of this thing. I could have done this [spreads his arms wide] and not touched a thing. I don't know what happened after that. I just remember thinking, shit, I got the worst cramp in my foot."

He had been swallowed inside the tube, and when he surfaced, he reached down to grab his left foot. "The thing was just shattered. I broke all the bones—every single one. They were stickin' right through the skin. I don't know how it happened, I guess the sheer compression of the wave did it. Nobody came to help me; it was too fuckin' big. I just crawled up the beach and they carted me off to town, because they couldn't deal with it out here." A plate of steel, since removed, was inserted in Nellis' foot. It took him nearly a year to recover.

"I'd like to re-live that wave," he says now. "I don't know, maybe it was just too hollow, but that day was absolute perfection—springtime conditions, and uncrowded. If that same wave came through again tomorrow, same angle, same size, I think I'd have to go. It was just too cool."

As the 1990s arrived, Nellis was working on his 19th consecutive winter on the North Shore. Although he actively avoids publicity, photographers and anything to do with a surf magazine, he's been paying attention. When I asked him about his favorite surfers over the years, he said, "I'd put Gerry Lopez at the top of the list. Incredible surfer, really good attitude, and he's got...I don't know, I don't want to sound mystical or anything, but Hawaiian surfers have a special feeling for the ocean. They can walk away from it for 5-10 years, pick up a surfboard, go out, and you'd never know it.

"Eddie [Aikau] was like that. I'll always remember his timing; he never got caught inside. Maybe you think all good surfers have that, but not here. That's a crock. Eddie knew when the big sets were coming, when to get out; he had *unreal* wave sense. Clyde's the same way. Perfect example. That guy hadn't been out at Waimea for years, but he went out there and won that contest [the first Eddie Aikau Invitational, in '86]. Everybody says it's because he's Eddie's brother? Horse *shit*. I can't even say if Eddie was better than Clyde. He'll go back and shut hole in that contest, and he'll be riding some pile-of-shit surfboard [laughs]. That'll make you love life, just to go and watch it.

"Lopez had a weird, catlike feel for waves, and he had the pure style out there. I remember this one time, I watched a guy completely burn him at Pipeline. Really bad. You think here's a skinny little guy, Lopez, he probably ain't too tough. Think again. This guy will ride a 20-foot barrel, and he's afraid of *you?* I don't think so. So he takes this guy aside and gives him a lecture. Right in the water. Gerry completely chewed him out, but very calmly, and then he explained what to do. Didn't beat him up, nothin'. That's the classiest thing I ever saw. I learned a lot from that."

As for the other surfers from Nellis' early years, "Rory Russell was phenomenal. Rode small or big waves, with timing that could beat the devil. Either he was there or the waves came to him—one or the other. He was a guy who could surf two-foot Pupukea, and in that same afternoon go out and rip Waimea Bay. And I mean, really get on it. I always enjoyed surfing with that guy. Sam Hawk, Owl Chapman, those were guys who knew *no* fear. Owl, I don't know... he just lost it; thought he was a fuckin' rock star. But I have a respect in my heart for what he's done. He was out there riding huge Pipeline before Bradshaw even got here. Charging it. So I'll never talk him down. If someone rides big waves, to me, that's the true statement.

"For all-around surfers, Michael Ho is the best alive right now. I put Michael way ahead of his younger brother, any of 'em. And Derek's hot. He's *real* good, OK? But he ain't as good as Michael. He gets a whole lot more coverage—why? Because they're tired of lookin' at Michael. They've been lookin' at that little joker since he was 12 years old [laughs], winning the *mene-*

hune contests. He *can't* be good any more. But you put 'em both in the water, Michael's gonna shut his hole. He's just that much more agile. He has that much more sack."

Nellis can appreciate someone like Jim Soutar, the North Shore's head lifeguard and a big-wave rider with his own way of doing things. "All I see him doing is riding this handboard," says Nellis. "So I go, 'Hey Jim, I hardly see you surfing any more. What'd you do, hang it up?' He says, 'No, no, just waiting for the right day to go surfing.' Makes no sense to me, but it's perfectly logical to him. Now I see him out at Rocky Point, 6-8 feet, and that's gigantic Rocky Point. He's riding this handboard, just having a great time, when he could be surfing. But he's waiting for the right day. Who knows what it is? Maybe it'll be five years down the road, but it won't bother him a bit. That's the great thing about these guys. They don't let anything get 'em down."

Among friends, Nellis is known for his hilarious put-downs of the modern-day surf scene. I heard him get into it one night, over a few beers, and there's no point indicating "laughter," because it was constant. It wasn't the bitter tirade of some has-been, but a classic rip job from a surfer with all sorts of credentials.

"You think about the older surfers for a minute," he said. "They didn't have no fuckin' helicopters, weather reports, they didn't have shit for surfboards, no leashes...hey. That takes a *lotta* sack. They didn't even know the breaks that well! As far as being tied to a board out there, that sucks. First time I tried a leash on the North Shore, I hit the bottom for the first time ever. I'd much rather see it go back to no leashes. I mean, Jocko's [the ultra-shallow spot between Chun's and Laniakea] is crowded now. Before, you had a certain board just for Jocko's. It was the one under the house, just completely mutilated. You went out there when you'd had a few beers and didn't care. Same with Rocky Point. Boards just got *demolished* out there. Honolua [on Maui] was really something, before cords. You'd fly over, surf, and if you wiped out once, you had to go home. No exaggeration. That sheer cliff took care of everything.

"The actual act of surfing is a really pure and great thing. The rest of it is just a bunch of garbage. Maybe it's hypocritical for me to say, because I make surfboards for a living, but you ain't gonna find me walkin' around like some businessman. It's like I don't really exist. They say I'm sacrificing too much by spending a lot of time in the water, but I feel exactly the opposite. Those guys wind up going full circle. They chase money until it piles up so big, they have to spend it all to regress to where they were happy before. I'd rather eat coconuts, be a street person, before I do that.

"The business of surfing, the sponsorship and the photos, is just disgusting. They just pick their little sweetheart. Like, 'Here you go, you're gonna ride for us now. Let's take pictures . . . oh, we don't like that pink, we're gonna get you on an orange board now.' And I guess that's supposed to look cool on some of the fags you see wearing 'em. But see, out in the water, everybody's naked. There's a lot of guys who'll put you in your place real fast. I mean, you can send all the pro surfers in the world out to Sunset Beach, and then you put Butch Perreira out there, and he'll stand out. He's that good. The guy has four kids, works the night shift at the Kui Lima, but the business of surfing can't go out there with him, because he just completely shuts hole. What's your pink wetsuit doin' for you now? I worked 'til 4 this morning, and here I am, makin' you look bad, dude. And of course, the photographers ain't gonna take no pictures of Butch.

"Hey, Shaun Tomson, Mark Richards, those guys are really hot. Tom Curren just rips; he don't need no photographers. But I can't believe some of the stuff goin' on now. Pro surfers just come over here and whine — they ain't gettin' enough photos in the magazines, they ain't got their check in the mail, they don't have a girlfriend. This one guy, a supposedly pro surfer, actually told me he doesn't want to ride big waves. I said, 'Christ, drop nut and get out there.' Another guy's talking about this contest he's missing in California for whatever-much money. And I'm thinkin', you'll give up *this* so you can go lose in that contest, get your picture taken, or get your name written as a mention on Surfer Notes in the back of the Butt-Plug issue? I mean, give me a break."

Nellis stopped for a moment, and finally admitted, "There might be just a little jealousy built up in me because these guys have it so easy. But what I had, I wouldn't trade for what they have in a million years. No way. Not what I've experienced."

And it's not just the great days. There are times when the North Shore simply wins, and you lose. Like all of the genuine big-wave surfers over the years, Nellis can talk about fear just as easily as conquest. "Sometimes you just know you've got to come in," he says. "I call it cold feet. It's an insecure feeling. You ain't got it any more. And if you're out there with cold feet, you're a hazard to everybody else in the water. Get the hell out of there. No shame. You're a goner. I get that feeling at Sunset sometimes, on 10-foot days. All of a sudden you find yourself backing out of waves you should be riding. Maybe it's fatigue, your adrenalin is gone, and you've come to your senses. You should *never* let somebody talk you into going out there, anywhere, unless you really want to. Because you're just gonna get killed. I mean, real dead.

"There was this one big swell when everybody was surfing Waimea, but me and Jim Booth were down at Haleiwa. And it was incredible: double-thick, dirty brown water, 12 feet plus. It's very, very rare that you can surf Haleiwa that big. I'm sittin' out there, and I've already wiped out two times. And with me, the third time's the charm. I'm outa there. So I get that weird feeling: 'I can't ride these waves.' And I look at Booth and say, 'Does it look like I've got CAUGHT INSIDE written across my forehead?' He says, 'Funny you should mention that. I've got the same feeling.' So I whipped around and took off, but Booth stayed out, and sure enough, he just got drilled. He came in, we went and had lunch, and we went back out later, it was OK. You screw around for a while, stretch your scrotum, get it back together. But believe me, as soon as you get that feeling you don't belong, hey...you *don't* belong."

Nellis gets that feeling when Waimea Bay starts closing out, but on Super Bowl Sunday, 1988—the day Darrick Doerner caught one of the biggest waves in recent memory—Nellis caught his all-timer, too. "I was walkin' down the beach when Darrick got that wave, and it was pushing 30 feet. It was the biggest wave I've seen that was really ridden well. I went, fuck, I'm out there. I remember Bill Sickler, Bradshaw and Brock Little being out when I was. I was surprised we even *got* out. I was just sittin' there going, 'Whoa. This is wild.' Guys were sitting in the channel, and that was *not* far enough. Over there, you were in danger of gettin' caught inside by the *left*. Everybody's kind of staring at one another, but no one's ridin'. Guys were paddling, but you just knew they weren't gonna go. Finally this one came in, and I just went, *voila.* This is it. I was the only guy to take off during the time I was out there. And I just got the peter bent on me."

Nellis got to the bottom of that wave, a solid 25-footer. In fact, he rode it across the bay. But he really paid the price, because a 30-foot wave was breaking outside. "I know it was 30 feet, because it landed on me [laughter]. It had broken a ways out, but it just blew the daylights out of me. Even when I came up, I had to dig myself a hole through this incredibly thick foam on top. And somehow [with no leash], my board was right there. I just got on that thing, held on, got washed up the beach, went to Foodland, got myself a six-pack, and watched the rest of the guys who never took off."

Like that day at Pipeline, when his foot broke into little pieces, Nellis found himself re-living the wave and the horrendous consequence of being caught inside. "That Pipeline wave, I'd definitely take off on that one again. It was definitely worth it," he said.

"The one at Waimea, I'm not so sure."

He stopped and thought for a moment.

"Yeah, I would."

Mark Cunningham

In the mid-1950s, when a pioneering group of Hawaiians and Californians started surfing the North Shore in earnest, the place was more mystique than reality. Surfers had a difficult time just *finding* Haleiwa and Sunset Beach in those days, and they were never sure what they were getting into. There's the classic, chilling story of the three surfers riding Sunset at 10 feet, then 15, then 18, and finally so big they had to bail out. Frightened at the prospect of trying to paddle in, they figured Waimea Bay — some three miles to the south — would be the better call. As darkness fell, two of those surfers staggered wearily onto the beach — but the third, Dickie Cross, didn't make it.

"That's the kind of story I grew up with on the East side," says 34-year-old Mark Cunningham. "And it was no fabrication. Those things happened. Still do."

Now, try this: As dawn breaks, Pipeline is pumping in at 12-15 feet—pretty much the maximum and, realistically, closer to 25 feet if you're out there. There's a solitary figure walking toward the ocean, toting only a pair of swim fins, and with nobody around—not even on the beach—he goes bodysurfing. That was Mark Cunningham, day after big day after ridiculous day, throughout the 1980s.

"I had countless sessions out there that nobody even knows about," he says. "Early morning, late evening, in the middle of a thunderstorm, when everyone else was huddled around their cocoa and color TV. I'd have big, wild-ass Pipeline with lightning goin' off, just loving it to death."

No matter how often I mention Cunningham's name around North Shore surfers, the reaction is the same: a vigorous nod, then a disbelieving shake of the head, and a comment like, "*That* guy...."

"That guy," says Tom Nellis, "is a *bitch*. He's incredible, just inhuman. I mean, wait a minute, *bodysurfing* big Pipeline? And he gets in the tube and comes out! Skinny as a ricket, too—like a strong wind would blow him over."

As he strides up the beach, 6-4 and 170 pounds, Cunningham has a timeless look. He could be 22, or 42, but whatever it is, he's primed. He was a pretty fair water polo player in his collegiate days at UC Santa Barbara, and some feel he could have been an Olympic swimmer. Instead, Cunningham chose Pipeline. He's been a full-time lifeguard there since 1978, and he's been bodysurfing it longer than that. Seen it all, done it all. He'd never say it himself, but Mark Cunningham *is* Pipeline.

"He's just wild out there, totally wild," says fellow North Shore lifeguard Rick Williams, a first-rate surfer and Hawaii resident since 1974. "He knows exactly how to get out, how to get in, which waves to pick, which to let go, and when to pull out [laughs]. That's the biggest thing. When it comes to taking off on a 10-foot wave without a board, going right over that ledge, with that kind of bottom... this guy's pretty talented. Pretty fearless. I've been out there [surfing] at 8 feet, and I just can't force myself over a ledge like that.

"You can tell Mark's style, and he'll generally ride farther than anyone else," said Williams. "He conforms more with the wave than the other guys, rides higher in the pocket. If you see somebody riding all the way across, chances are it's him. He doesn't do a lot of spinners and trick stuff, like the guys at Point Panic and Sandy Beach. He's just getting into the tightest spot, bending his body to fit the wave, and making it out."

The North Shore lifeguards are truly an elite crew. Darrick Doerner is probably riding more 20-foot waves, consistently and well, than any surfer in the world. Jimmy Blears is a huge name in the sport, going back to the late '60s. Terry Ahue, Cunningham's partner at Pipeline, has been known to paddle out through Beach Park, cruise past Pupukea and Rocky Point, on to Kammieland, and finally arrive at Sunset for water patrol. Williams is a champion paddler, Ted Lowdermilk a world-class bodysurfer, Mike Garrity one of the hottest young surfers around...it goes on and on.

Cunningham, though, might have the best reputation. He's saved hundreds of lives over the years, too many to count, and many more than the record shows. "If you were to check our lifeguard files in Honolulu, all the rescue reports with the name 'Cunningham' on them, you'd have maybe a third of the actual rescues I made," he says. "The guards here aren't real keen on paperwork. We're here to save lives and ride waves. Every now and then, we'll go through the formality of it."

That says a lot about Cunningham. He could have done a lot of things the proper way, the expected way, but he wouldn't have enjoyed the rip-roaring lifestyle he carved out for himself. For one thing, he doesn't look or sound like the average North Shore character. His mother and father, who worked for the Federal Aviation Agency, were both from Massachusetts; Mark was born there. You picture him going through prep school, the Ivy League, maybe wearing a crisp white suit at the local yacht club. He speaks slowly, deliberately—I heard him get four syllables out of "back then"—and intelligently, with sort of a Yale-goes-Makapuu accent. "People think I'm Austrian, or Australian—God, I've heard it all, and they don't know where I got my accent from," he says. "I can't explain it. Maybe it's this big beak I've got in the middle of my face [laughs]. Adds sort of a nasal twang to it."

I told him it sounded a bit East-Coast prep school. "Well, thank you, that's a compliment, I think," he said. "I thank my parents for that, teaching me manners and common courtesy.

It makes things so much more civilized and pleasant. Here in the surfing community, people are amazed that I talk as well as I do. Surfers are more known for, like, 'Unreal, man. This fuckin' unreal set came through.' And I slip into that sometimes, because I'm surrounded by it, and I probably slip into pidgin, too. I'm *sure* I do. You drink a few with the mates in the backyard, you start throwin' some 'bloodys' around. With the bruddas, you throw a little pidgin around."

Mark uses the word "jaded" to describe his outlook on North Shore life, and he's not always the friendliest guy you've run across. There's a visible strain in his face, from years of squinting into the late-afternoon sun, watching the lives of surfers and tourists endangered, and on the darkest days, holding a wounded or deceased person in his arms. You can run the whole deal past Mark Cunningham, and you won't be breaking much news.

On one particular February afternoon, I had a chance to spend a few hours with Cunningham behind his familiar tower at Ehukai Beach Park. The conditions were sunny and inviting, maybe 2-3 feet, and though he kept one eye on the surf, he generously ran down some details of his life in the islands.

He was conceived on Oahu, which somehow seems significant, and his parents moved there permanently when Mark was just two months old. "My dad had been stationed here right after World War II, and when he came back, he worked air traffic control on the outer islands. I grew up in Niu Valley, just 10 minutes away from Sandy Beach. That's where I learned how to bodysurf."

Niu Valley was quite a neighborhood. Cunningham's first house was just four doors away from Gerry Lopez. "Randy Rarick is from there, Dennis Pang, a lot of excellent surfers. I read all the magazines—you know, Joey Cabell and Mike Doyle, Kimo Hollinger, Sammy Lee, Paul Strauch and the 'cheater five'—and the thing about Hawaii is, you read about these guys, then you see 'em at the supermarket or the beach. You get to identify your idols as real people."

He wanted to be a ripping, stand-up surfer in the worst way. "I never really got there," he says. "I'm not fast at all, not quick enough leaping to my feet, the way you have to on the North Shore. Here I am at the greatest wave in the world, watching surfers just annihilate the place, and I still surf like a kook [laughter, as he pounds a fist on the sand]. I belong to the S.L.S.C.—the Statue of Liberty Surf Club. Pretty stiff. But I tell ya, I'm having fun."

He's having it like few have ever known, anywhere in the surfing world. For years, before his debilitating injury, the great Buffalo Keaulana was considered the best bodysurfer in Hawaii. Not fancy or showy, but most definitely at one with the wave—riding it the farthest, with the most style. That title belongs to Mark Cunningham now, and let's just say it: If you're the best bodysurfer at Pipeline, you're the best. Period. Mark doesn't figure he'd do that well in California, because he's not used to weak, mushy waves or the reliance on trick maneuvers. But he also knows that in serious juice, as only Hawaii can bring it, he's going to be in charge.

"Somewhere along the line, Mark just made a commitment to bodysurfing," says Rarick. "I'm sure if he rode surfboards as much as he bodysurfed, he could have been a great surfer. But he made his choice, and it got him to the highest plane. I mean, I consider him one of the top ten guys I've ever seen at Pipeline—surfers, whatever. But before all that, I remember him on the East side, just day after day."

Cunningham vividly remembers the day it all came together for him. "It was my seventh-grade summer, out at Port Lock Point. There's this one little reef, sandwiched in between the coastline, where the beach is about 40 feet wide. On the right days, some nice rollers would come peeling in against the rocks, and that's where I got the first real sensation of riding, *staying* in a wave. That whole feeling of being so involved; your entire body being encompassed by this moving force. And on a real long ride, you just trim…and climb…and drop…and kind of trim again…and shit, I gotta come back *here* if I want to keep going...and yes, that works! God, just that sensation of the water flying by, rushing like a fire hose against my chest. Maybe that was the hook. When you're that low to the water, your sense of speed is just phenomenal. And it's not just riding the waves, it's swimming through them, it's diving under them, opening your eyes underwater as you watch this *thing* impact right in front of you. And you just knife right through there, between the bottom and where those whitewater fingers are tryin' to grab you. Just the whole dance out there. You're like a piece of the ocean. I mean, what is the human body made of? Water. The physical makeup of the bodily fluids and the ocean is very similiar. And now you've found each other. Hop on now, man, or you'll miss the train."

It took a long, rich education at places like Sandy Beach and Makapuu before Cunningham was ready for Pipeline. The place still seemed like a trek into the unknown, and he knew he'd have to make a full commitment to bodysurfing before attempting the place. "I was an All-American kid growing up in the suburbs. I had about a 10-year career in youth baseball. But when I got to 13, 14 years old, the surf bug hit —and hit hard, baby. I'm standing out in left field on some hot summer day, flagging down fly balls, when I knew there was a south swell goin' off and I could be out there surfing. Back then, the North Shore didn't make much sense. I didn't have a car, or even a license, and there were plenty of waves in my own back yard. Why spend an hour and a half on the road when Makapuu was 10 minutes away?"

Finally, when Mark was in ninth grade at Punahou School, some friends took him to Pipeline. They started at Off the Wall, then gradually moved over into the prime-time break. "The one sensation I'll always remember from that first day— and it's still one of my strongest feelings from all my years of wave-riding—were those first couple of rides. Getting my breathing down. Where I came from, once you knew the wave was gonna shut down, you did your little tuck-and-roll pullout. On these waves, I'd see the lip start coming over me, hold my breath, sort of waiting for the 'thump!' to come…and I'd still be riding. And the tube would be comin' over me. *Still* riding. And I'd be running out of air, so I'd take another breath real quick. *Still* in the tube, and I'm out of breath again! This went on, wave after wave. It was so amazing, the hang time you had in there. Every now and then I'd come out of one, which was really unbelievable. It blew me away."

Cunningham graduated from Punahou in 1974, his reputation now starting to build. I asked Mark about his early contest record, and he sort of shrugged it off, not that anxious to discuss it. But I really wanted to know. "I hate to sound egotistical," he said. "But I pretty well hands-down dominated. Just cleaned clock on junior men's. Sandy's, Makapuu, Point Panic, and finally over at Pipeline. A lot of the senior men were thankful I wasn't in their division."

Cunningham didn't know the meaning of "slump," because he never had one. He dominated from the very beginning, at every level. He figures he hasn't lost more than two or three contests, ever, in waves of any consequence. "I won the first contest I entered, when I was 17, at Sandy's. In my second contest at Makapuu, I lost out in a semifinal heat. And that was really good, it gave me a dose of humility. But damn it, I didn't let it happen again."

In those days, a lot of Hawaiian kids were heading to California—UCLA, Cal, Stanford, Santa Barbara—to swim and play water polo. Cunningham wasn't so sure about leaving the islands, but he decided to play water polo under Dante Dettemanti (later one of the sport's most highly regarded coaches) at UCSB. "I wasn't the full-on Nazi water polo player that schools like Cal and UCLA were producing," he said. "Santa Barbara sounded good, and I played for the freshman team. I also got my first real coaching in swimming, all the mechanics and fine points, and I got a whole new lease on life. Just the pure rhythm of kicking, where to put your hands in and out of the water, breathing out of the corner of your mouth instead of jerking your head, all that fine-tuning.

"I came back in the best shape of my life, and it made bodysurfing *so* much more pleasurable. It was like I'd been driving a Porsche with the parking brake on, for all those years. My high-school coach had always been on me to swim, but no dice, babe, I'm going to Sandy Beach. I'm not really ready to go back and forth in a chlorine dip, looking at the bottom of a pool."

Cunningham moved up to the UCSB varsity in '75, and he hooked up with the Santa Barbara City lifeguard department. But when he came home for the Christmas holidays that winter, his father was gravely ill with cancer. He would last only two more months. Mark made the decision to stay home with his mother and two sisters for a while, and he never returned to California. "I wasn't cutting it scholastically, to be honest. I was just physically exhausted. I don't see how people can be full-fledged, semipro athletes at a major college and get an education at the same time. It just baffles me. Let's face it, I was an island boy. I'd had my California experience, and damned if I didn't want to get home to this.

"I never did get back to school. I kicked around the community colleges in Honolulu, but I was just going through the motions. What am I doing in school? Pipeline could be perfect today. What am I doing trying to discuss philosophy with a bunch of Orientals who are so shy they can barely speak?"

In the summer of '76, Cunningham was hired as a lifeguard by the city and county of Honolulu. "They only hired a few guards that summer, and thank God for water polo, I aced the swim test," he said. He worked the West side, and Sandy's, and by the winter of that year he had a Pipeline trial. "Butch Van Artsdalen was the head guard out here then, and Terry Ahue, my partner now, was working with him. But Butch didn't stick around long. [A heavy drinker and Pipeline surfing legend, Van Artsdalen died of cirrhosis of the liver in July of '79.] The lifeguard who really pulled me in was Sean Ross."

There's a key name. I'd seen Ross in the late '70s, pulling off miracles in big Pipeline with nothing but a flat sheet of wood. "Absolutely the best paipo boarder *ever* in big waves," Cunningham said. "In those days, only Lopez and Rory Russell were spending more time in the tube out at Pipeline. Sean was a real inspiration to me. He wanted a physically fit partner that he could work with. When the shit hits the fan out here, you want some backup, baby, someone you can *count* on. For a summer or two I'd go back to Sandy's, because it gets flat as a lake out here, but in August of '78 I became a full-time guard at Pipeline."

He was eminently ready for the task. They held the Lightning Bolt Professional Bodysurfing Championships in big, onshore conditions in December of 1980, and as Bernie Baker wrote in *Surfer*, "If you sat and watched the finals, you would have sworn that it wasn't Mark out there, but a porpoise taking off from underwater, free-falling with the section and planing out into the flats, all the way down to Beach Park. When Mark was announced the winner, the rest of the competition picked him up and carried him back down to the water for a congratulatory dumping. It was more than just friendship or sheer elation; it was family."

Part of that competition was Californian Mike Cunningham, one of the world's great bodysurfers in his own right. "We've been mistaken for one another for years," says Mark. "We're known as twin brothers, I believe, in some circles. He was playing polo at UCLA when I was at Santa Barbara, and he's a full-time lifeguard for L.A. County. He's been extremely successful in the Oceanside contests."

The thrill of dominating the Hawaiian circuit began diminishing for Mark after a while. "I was going to the same beaches, against the same competition, and it kind of lost its glamour, its appeal. I didn't need any more funky plastic trophies. In the back of my mind I'd be thinking, 'Well, if you're the best, see if you can become a professional bodysurfer.' But I never pursued it. I figured if somebody wanted me for that, they knew where to find me. It wasn't in my character to approach someone with a resume and tell 'em how great I was, what I could do for their product.

"I could feel this pressure: 'Come on, Mark, do it for the rest of us. Open some doors. Get some money involved in the sport.' But I didn't want to play that game. I just wanted to go surfing. I'm sure a lot of people said, 'God, what a dumb fuck' [laughter], but I never wanted to whore myself. In my own mind, you know? I've never been sponsored by anybody. And it's not like there's a whole lot to endorse. You've got your trunks, and you've got your fins, and Duck Feet and Churchill had that market cornered. [Cunningham wears Duck Feet and fins of that style, having never appreciated the Churchill design.] I just think bodysurfing is a real special sort of deal, just you and the ocean. The rest of that scene, forget it."

Cunningham took a house on the Pipeline beachfront in the early '80s, and he spent the rest of the decade there. He became familiar with Pipeline's insanely courageous underground, the likes of Adam Salvio, Bruce Hansel, Brian Bulkley, Doug Brown, Jim Ingham, Bob Fram, Tony Roy and Mickey Neilsen. "Every surfer puts in a little time here, but most of 'em would rather be someplace else," he says. "Off the Wall or Sunset, maybe on the West side or something. So I really respect the guys who put in time here.

"Bruce Hansel is right at the top of the list. A real soft-spoken fellow who just loves to surf big, nasty Pipeline. He and Bulkley were partners in crime for many years out there. Any time Gerry or Rory would come, of course, they would shine. But for a couple of years, Bulkley and Bruce were the dominators out there. Just wild men. We've carried Bruce up this beach a number of times. And Adam Salvio—we call him Adam-12— there's a real special guy. I can't count the number of times it was just the two of us in really wild conditions."

"Mark's the only guy who would be out there after dark with me," says Salvio. "I'd see him sit out on the second reef, then bodysurf right into the inside bowl. He'd go on waves we *wouldn't* go on. I surfed Pipeline with Jose Angel, and I surfed it with Lopez. Cunningham is in that category. Their presence in the water keeps it together. It gets chaotic when they aren't around."

Cunningham grew up near Lopez, watched him in his prime, "and he still cuts the prettiest line out there. People may have ridden as deep, or as well, but never as consistently. No one has, no one ever will. It's interesting, you can see Gerry's style in Derek Ho. Derek's the king, the new Man at Pipeline, and you can see that easy-does-it style, going with the flow, let's not get too worked up about things. Poor Derek, he's got that pure Hawaiian upbringing going against the rip-and-tear, slash-and-splash attitude of the ASP circuit. That's a real dilemma. I'm sure the kid has a tough time balancing that act. But God, it sure is a pleasure to watch him draw that clean, easy, effortless line at Pipeline. I'll be real curious to see if Derek's out there in 10 years. I'll be curious to see if *I'm* out there."

Another pure Hawaiian touch is that when perfect waves arrive, little else matters. He's a lifeguard, yes, but Cunningham has always enjoyed his share of Pipeline. "It depends how my partners are feeling, how generous they are," he says. "My being able to bodysurf that often is only because I have a solid, on-the-ball partner like Terry Ahue. He has that sixth sense, as all good lifeguards do, of something happening —when and where. He's a very quiet, heroic man. I'm honored to have had him with me for so many years. We have to make sure everybody's gonna be OK on the sandbar before we get in our water time."

Cunningham is amazed there aren't more deaths at Pipeline. "On those big days, you'll sit here and watch hundreds of bad wipeouts. Just tons and tons of water, slamming down on what amounts to a parking lot. But you know it's bound to happen. Someone's head is gonna connect, real hard.

"I remember one sunny Saturday, Pipe was fairly crowded, 6-8 feet. I wasn't on duty. I ran into Don King, who's a fantastic swimmer, and he was checking the place out for photos.

Suddenly there was a board dancing in the whitewater. And a wave washes over it, and it doesn't roll in. Another wave hits it ...kind of stays there. And I said, 'Don, I think somebody's at the other end of that.' I'm in a pair of corduroy shorts with parachute pockets, no fins or tube or anything; I just hopped in the current.

"I get to the board, and I start...it's the worst feeling... pulling up this cord. Who's it going to be? And it's so absurd, because the first thing you pull out is a foot. Of course, that's what's attached to a leash. But you've got to see what's at the other end of this. It was a young boy, a teenager, from the other side of the island. I tried to give him a couple of quick breaths, and it was so difficult with all that water moving around, with no fins on. Finally I straddled him somehow, and tried to blow on him. There was a cut, right across his throat, and my breath just went, shhoo! Right out the windpipe.

"Don was right behind me, and we were sitting there realizing we had a dead kid on our hands. This isn't like television, gang, where it's lifeguard to the rescue. You lose 'em sometimes. I think we both said a mutual prayer right then for the guy. God, coming in through six-foot Ehukai shorebreak, you're just happy not to lose the body. There is no life to be saved; just get the corpse in. First thing we hear is the screaming girlfriend, who recognizes his board, and her dead boyfriend is there on the beach."

There was a long pause. Mark was just staring out to sea.

"There was another one, a kid from Haleiwa named Dan Gora, born and raised on the North Shore. He went out surfing right before dark, when the guards were getting off work, on a good-sized day, 6-8 feet. I remember seeing him pull into the parking lot with his buddy. He'd been working all day, and he was stoked.

"The sun was going down, and he never came in. I remember the helicopter searching that night, and it was a solid eight feet—a Hawaiian eight feet. I was out bodysurfing with Ted Lowdermilk the next morning. We looked back at the beach and said, 'What are all those people doing at Beach Park?' Turned out it was Dan's family, hoping to see his remains. That was such a strange feeling, being out there, having a killer time in the surf, and there was a family grieving on the beach. I didn't know the details until I came in. Later that day, the body washed in off Ke Waena.

"I couldn't even give you an estimate on the years of those deaths," he said. [I could have checked, but I couldn't really see the point.] "There have been others, too. It's almost the kind of thing you block out of your mind. It's just my makeup, or maybe all the dope I smoked in my earlier years [laughter], but...it's just something you don't want to remember. You've seen millions of waves, and millions of wipeouts, and tens of thousands of beautiful girls, saved hundreds and hundreds of lives...."

And yes, you get jaded. The best part about Mark Cunningham is that he's still around Pipeline—living in Nuuanu Valley now, with his stunning wife Linny, but still around. A comfortable, familiar presence. And still stoked on bodysurfing the place.

"I don't venture too far from here, because it gets the job done for me," he says. "This is the best bodysurfing on the island by far, and it doesn't have to be 8-10-foot Pipe for me. I'll be out there bodysurfing two-foot sandbar, and just diggin' on it. I wouldn't recommend Backdoor. I got stuck in one of the gullies [in the coral] once and *really* got held under for a while. I surfaced just in time to get impacted by the next wave, and I kind of rolled around on the sidewalk down there. That was many years ago, and I sat on the beach for a while, pretty shook up, with a new lesson learned and new-found respect for the spot. You haven't seen me out there since. But Banzai Rocks, over by Ke Waena, can be excellent. Pipe, Beach Park, Pupukea, it can all be great. No need for me to be anyplace else."

Let's talk about bodysurfing Pipeline for a minute. I've seen it done, and I'm a fair bodysurfer myself, but I can never get over the skill, timing and just plain guts required to ride that place. You couldn't pay my way out there in big surf.

"I know a few times some of the Wedge boys have come over from California, and they'll just kick right over that peak, and they're into this monster macho crash-and-burn kind of thing, you know? This is what bodysurfing is to them. I'm in it for long rides and longevity, baby. I'm gonna *make* that wave. This isn't a sand bottom we're talkin' about here, and some of those guys got pretty nailed. Now I'm hearing through the grapevine where they're bad-mouthing the place. But it's just a whole new deal. They're not used to such a vast area, or jockeying with the surfers."

Make no mistake, he says, "No bodysurfer can sit on the peak, make the drop and come through that initial section. You're a little bit off to the side, looking for a certain west peak that sort of pushes its way across, instead of just crashing top to bottom. I do a shitload of jockeying out there, without trying to be too obvious about it. I mean, I'm not out there talking about my last wave, or my latest endorsement deal, or where I was partying last night. I'm out there studying—the intervals, the swell direction, where the current's pulling the lineup, where it's pulling me—and I think I'm doing that a little harder than everyone else. It's just head level for a bodysurfer; I'm down in the chops and troughs of these waves. I *have* to concentrate harder. It's not that I'm trying to be a jerk, but excuse me, I'm trying to bodysurf out here.

"When I get that super-west wave that just pushes me across, I want to ride it as long as I can. That's the one thing that really drives me up the wall, when I see these rip-and-tear surfers out there, just aggro as they can be, grabbin' every wave they can. They shoot the tube, shake the water out of their head, kick out, and they're back in the lineup. I'm thinking, you prick, kick back—do a cutback, ride it into the reform, do an off-the-lip and come back down with the whitewater. I don't want to *see* you for a while. I mean, will you please get your money's worth and ride the damn thing to the beach? Give the rest of us a chance out here? It's really funny, because Lopez has been doing that for years, just milking his waves for all they're worth, enjoying them to the fullest. And no one picks up on it."

Regrettably, there is very little evidence of Cunningham's art. Despite his formidable status, he's been shamefully ignored by surf filmmakers and magazines. There is one recently released video, a 23-minute Honolulu production entitled "Waves to Freedom," that is devoted entirely to Cunningham. He's shown bodysurfing beautiful waves at Pipeline, Banzai Rocks and Waimea in the early '80s, when those spots were relatively uncrowded for bodysurfing. "In those days, when the conditions weren't quite right for surfers, I'd just be out there alone. There are too many bodyboarders now, just hanging around the fringe of the lineups. There's a mood to that video you just can't find today."

But the waves haven't changed. The sight of Cunningham at Pipeline, perfectly slotted in a 50-yard ride or longer, is truly unforgettable. "With the right swell direction, and the right amount of sand, it's a phenomenal wave. It's sucking you up the face, wanting to throw you over the falls, and gravity is pulling you down. You're just trimming along that face, trying to stay as high as you can, because that's where the speed line is. For a free-fall you need that extra momentum, where you're actually airborne and diving out. You'd better get all the momentum you can if you're gonna dive through the bottom of a Pipeline wave and make it out the back. The classic bodysurfer's mistake at Pipeline is like, all right, they made the drop, and then they just get stuffed down there, pinned like a dog. If you've made the drop, you'd better be able to get back up to the high part of the wave. Guys think they can get down and glide off the bottom? Oh, no. Nothin' doin'. There's no escape from that. You have *no* speed to dive out the back, and not enough to continue. You're at its mercy.

"The ideal Pipeline wave is a half-drop. I like to take off on an angle and start trimming as soon as I can. The top third of the wave, that's where all the speed is. I think in the past 10 years, I've been in the barrel out there more than anyone else, and as a bodysurfer, you don't come out of 'em nearly enough. But that's OK, because when you do, it makes it all the more special. It's Niagara Falls goin' off on one side of you, and the beautiful green wall suckin' up the opposite direction, and maybe some surfer's paddling out on the shoulder, making eye contact, and there's that stoke going through the air.

"I've been over the falls, lots and lots of times, but those are becoming fewer, because I just don't like to put myself in that situation any more. I want to be bodysurfing for a lot more years; I won't take off on nearly as many of the big, crazy-ass waves that I used to."

What *about* those big days? How does one possibly handle that? "You feel like you're sittin' on top of the world," he says. "You've got a beautiful sunrise or sunset, the fish and turtles swimming underneath you, this incredible coming together of the earth, sea and sky, and you get to feelin' real lucky and thankful and happy to be alive. Here you are at the most famous wave in the world, some of the best surfers are sitting on the beach, maybe not quite sure what to do, and you're out there with the place to yourself. Maybe you're not catching many, but you're breaking the ice.

"It's the solitude that gets me off, not [TV-announcer voice] *'The shallowest reef in the world, waiting to chew me up if I make one false move.'* No, that's the stuff of movies. Not for this kid. I'm out there for personal satisfaction, and I've gotten it. On a handful of big days over the years, when it's 12 feet and beyond, I've been at second reef and picked a few off. But you know, even if I hadn't... God, I had the best seats in the house."

Mike Stewart

I was heading south on the Kam Highway one dreary Thanksgiving morning when I stopped to check Pipeline. It was a wild, stormy 12 feet, with a mean little north hook to the swell, and there appeared to be nobody out. Just before walking away; I noticed a bodyboarder in the lineup. He pulled into a set wave, negotiated a near-impossible drop, cranked off the bottom and seemed to power his way through a collapsing section on the force of sheer will. He finally came careening out of the whitewater, rode the wave in, showered, and drove away. No friends, no fans, no sun, no cameras, no glory. This was Mike Stewart's idea of a leisurely morning.

There are times when you figure you've seen it all in this sport. Jack Lindholm's ground-breaking, drop-knee rides at huge Pipeline in the late '70s deserve a choice spot in history. Daniel Kaimi performed the first barrel rolls there in the early '80s. Keith Sasaki, Danny Kim, Tom Boyle and an up-and-coming group of Kauai riders are absolute standouts in Hawaiian surf. When the North Shore gets big, people like Hauoli Reeves, Pat Caldwell, Seamas Mercado, Phyllis Dameron, Carol Philips, Kai Santos, Dean Marzol, Kainoa McGee and Lindholm take over. Ben Severson combines the best of all these riders into a dynamite package, either in competition or free surfing. This is why Mike Stewart has such an incredible reputation on the North Shore, because he blows them *all* away. Occasionally, a magazine will suggest there's

93

some sort of race for No. 1 in the world, but there is no race. It's Mike Stewart up front, everybody else in the back.

Let's face it, unless the waves are either enormous or unusually good, bodyboarding can become tedious as a spectator sport. There are too many kids out there, all looking the same, doing their hopeless little spinners into eternity. "The gyro-spastic spinfest," as Sasaki describes it so vividly. It can be a pretty weak look, especially in the gladiator atmosphere of the North Shore.

"They're just a nuisance," Tom Nellis said bluntly, speaking on behalf of thousands of stand-up riders. "All they do is get in the way. They should all be run over and just driven out of the water."

A few of those other riders get respect, but Stewart seems to have transcended the sport. His performances at Pipeline have established him as one of the best *surfers*, period, in the world. I remember the first day I saw Mike at Pipe. It was around '84, on a huge day, and I was impressed to see this wiry, confident-looking kid come howling off the bottom without the benefit of a skeg. Then he rocketed toward the lip and pitched himself upside down, leaving himself a legitimate 20-foot free-fall into a section ravaged by whitewater. This was all part of the plan. He completed the 360-degree aerial, landed like a vintage Cessna 150 and continued riding, still in the wave. I'm a bodyboarder myself, been out in the waves since the mid-1950s, and I literally lost my balance at the sight of this maneuver. I just sort of crumbled to the sand. And when I started asking people about Stewart, now entering his prime at 27, I realized I wasn't alone.

Darrick Doerner: "The stuff I've seen him do is beyond extremes. Keith and Ben and those guys, they're excellent, but when Pipe gets big, out on the second reef, they're on the beach. Pipe is such a heavy place—it's so dangerous, I don't even surf it any more—and Mike's got more guts than anybody else out there. He's a master, one in a million, like a Robbie Naish, Tommy Curren or Mario Andretti."

Mike Latronic: "He gets deeper at Off the Wall tubes than anybody I've ever seen. He's just back there playing with the foam."

Mark Cunningham: "In the future, people will realize that he's in the same league as Gerry Lopez, Derek Ho and the other Pipeline Masters champions. I can see it already. I hate to use silly words like 'phenomenal' and 'awesome,' but the guy really is head and shoulders above everyone else out there. I mean, on one of those nasty 12-15-foot days, he's sitting farther back than the top ASP board riders, and he's spending more time in the tube than any of them. A lot of people in the surfing industry say, 'Oh, God, he's on his stomach, anyone can flop around like that.' Bullshit. They can't. Not the way he's doing it. It's like a big stage, and Mike's just dancing all over it."

Photographer Don King: "I've seen him do that off-the-lip rollo where he went 40, 50 feet through the air. Hit the water and didn't lose a moment. He's doing things that nobody else is doing, and he's pulling it off in the heaviest, most dangerous waves anywhere. To me, that makes him the best surfer in the world."

Coming from King, one of the North Shore's best water men, that's quite a statement. A controversial one, too. "If a bodyboarder is a surfer, then so is a bodysurfer and a tandem rider and a jet-skier, OK?" says North Shore aficionado Bernie Baker. "You and I know what a surfer is. But Mike Stewart is the best tube rider in the world, and I don't think another surfer will ever touch him. It has to do with his center of gravity, being able to make lane adjustments on his craft. He's not dealing with kneecaps, shock absorbers or catching rails. He can make all those fine adjustments. If his center of gravity were any lower, he'd be a skin diver."

The "best surfer" argument is really sort of pointless. "That's like asking, who's the most beautiful woman?" said Randy Rarick. "Is Rachel Ward more beautiful than Bo Derek? I mean, you watch Gerry Lopez coming out of a barrel, and what could be better than that? But Mike is like what Tom Curren was a couple of years ago. The best overall in his field."

Surfer Magazine once published a gallery of photos labeled "The Gun Club." It showed a variety of established surfers alongside their big-wave guns: Peter Cole, Keone Downing, Flippy Hoffman, Ken Bradshaw, Richard Schmidt, the whole shot. And there was Stewart, the only bodyboarder in the crowd. More recently, *Surfer* polled an elite group of surfers to determine the current Top Ten at Pipeline. Stewart finished ninth, right in there with Derek Ho, the late Ronnie Burns, Tom Carroll, Lopez, Johnny Boy Gomes, Dane Kealoha, Michael Ho, Marvin Foster and Max Medeiros.

Jon Damm, one of the very best at Pipe, listed Stewart No. 1—*then* Derek Ho and Burns. "What he's doing out there is just inhuman," said Damm. "He's just blown people's doors off—even with his paddling. We're pretty good paddlers, and this guy makes us look silly. Just say my girlfriend's a body-boarder, and Mike's her hero."

After all this praise, after a career unblemished by failure, you'd think Mike would be pretty impressed with himself. Sort of strutting around, like, "Am I unreal, or what?" On the contrary, he comes off as a polite, unpretentious beach kid, with the pure-stoke enthusiasm of a surfer who has just seen Hawaii for the first time. "Those comments are really flattering to me," he says. "It's beyond flattery. There's no way I'd try to take advantage of that, or use it for wrong. Hey, in certain conditions I'm the worst guy in the water. On a small day at Rocky Point, there's only so much I can do. But if you get into conditions that are just absurdly heavy, I might excel more than the rest. I do know this: Never think you have a total edge over anyone, because you don't. The second you think you have it wired is the second you go down."

In Cunningham's words, "Mike's not doing it for macho bravado or to prove anything. He gets real satisfaction from it. Some of the articles focus on Mike Stewart the mystery man,

Mark Cunningham: North Shore lifeguard, Pipeline authority, and big-wave bodysurfer of the highest order

Cunningham's ability to get to the bottom at Pipeline is a constant source of amazement

Mike Stewart at his best, setting up for the tube at Pipeline

Above, Stewart's local knowledge gives
him a takeoff to himself at Pipeline.
Back home on the Big Island, left,
Stewart hiked two miles across freshly-
cooled volcanic lava to find waves.

Stewart has been called the best surfer in the world. There's plenty of evidence.

Cunningham, high line on a West peak. "That's where all the speed is."

Craig Fineman, Surfer Magazine

Marvin Foster at second-reef Pipeline. The wave won't stay casual for long.

Art Brewer, Surfer Magazine

Bobby Owens, Waimea Bay. For serious riders only.

Michael Ho, a Hawaiian surfing master under any conditions

Mike Latronic, showing his years of experience at Sunset

Rob Gilley, Surfer Magazine

Women don't ride the biggest waves — but how big do you want?
Margo Oberg, Sunset.

Bernie Baker

Lynne Boyer, stylish and aggressive at Sunset

Phyllis Dameron (above and right, at Waimea). "She's out there because she loves it."

Carol Philips: A bodyboarding standout in big surf

Brian Bielmann

Craig Fineman

Ronnie Burns had a passion for high-speed dirt biking. In July of 1990, he met his death on the trails above the North Shore. One of the truly great Hawaiian surfers at any spot, particularly Pipeline, Burns was just 27 years old. He will be missed.

this incredibly analytical competitor-scientist. I just call Mike a Hawaiian. He has that real soulful side of appreciating the beauty of nature, and 15-foot Pipeline is one of her faces. He's out there because he truly loves it."

The scientist angle comes from Mike's computer, a portable lap-top that he takes on tour with him around the world. Using a modem and random number generator, he keeps everything in there: daily diaries, letters, phone numbers, maneuvers he's attempted, some others he's planning. And most of all, his contest record. You'd *need* a computer for that—and a cash register, while you're at it.

It's pretty astounding, really. Aside from winning seven of the nine major contests held at Pipeline, Stewart completely dominated the PSAA pro tour in 1987-88-89. He reached the finals in 79 consecutive contests—something akin to Joe DiMaggio's 56-game hitting streak—before getting eliminated in a bland Santa Cruz semifinal in May of '89. Even in small waves, the great equalizer without the factor of fear, Stewart keeps his edge. And make no mistake, while he has a kind, gentle nature and a traditionalist's attitude toward surfing, he's a ruthless, almost maniacal competitor in contests.

"You see him day-to-day, and he's just a real friendly, goofball sort of guy," says Boyle, probably the leading authority on bodyboarding through his writing, surfing and photography. "Then he puts on a heat jersey, and it's all over. You're just shooting for second place. I've seen him try to actually catch every wave in a contest—a phenomenal feat. His drive to win is almost scary."

During the 1986 Morey contest, held in 8-10-foot conditions that had some international competitors trembling, "Mike just psyched everybody out," said Boyle. "He was *laughing.* 'I'm gonna have a field day out here,' he says, just to check out the other guys' reactions. I remember this one huge set came in, and Mike gets this horrified look in his eyes, starts paddling as fast as he can. The other guys start paddling frantically. Then Mike just stopped. He was laughing so hard, he nearly fell off his board. He was *toying* with people."

The more his rivals hear about Stewart, the more depressed they get. "There are all sorts of rumors about me," he says, but they are based on fact. Such as:

● He doesn't wear a leash, and he's one of the best bodysurfers in Hawaii. "Oh, easily," says Cunningham. "He's one of the few people that will come up to me on a full-moon evening and go, 'Mark, tonight's the night. Let's go do it.'" One night, as Stewart and Don King headed out for some Pipeline bodysurfing, they noticed one of the outside reefs going off at Rocky Point. Then Pipe's second reef started feathering. "Let's get out there quick, before we have any second thoughts," Stewart told King. And they launched themselves into a few big shoulders in the dark. Stewart takes pride in his bodysurfing, and his ability seems limitless. In the 1991 Pipeline context, a red-hot event featuring Cunningham, King and Severson, Stewart stole the title with a performance that sent everyone back to the drawing board. Time and again, he pulled off the 360 barrel roll without the benefit of a board, getting right back into the wave. "Never seen anything like it," said Cunningham.

● Stewart may have saved King's life on a surfing trip to Grajagan, Java. The two of them were cranking through surf in a 15-horsepower Zodiac, just playing around, when an off-the-lip maneuver sent both of them flying. "The boat got stuck on full throttle," King recalled. "It started zooming around in circles like a mad hornet, bouncing on the chop." In a gutty move, Stewart stuck his body in front of the boat and the propeller nicked his hand. "Would have chopped it right off if it were three inches higher in the water," said King. "Then the boat started heading out to sea, jumping waves. I figured it was gone. Then it turned around and came right back at us. Mike goes, 'Your turn.' I sort of tackled the thing and grabbed on, but my legs were getting sucked down toward the prop. Mike jumped in and shut the motor down. If he hadn't done that, I don't think I could have hung on."

• On a trip to Indonesia, as Boyle tells it, "Mike and I were standing there watching Uluwatu at about 11-12 feet. A bunch of surfers were lying around getting their massages, talking about how incredible Padang Padang had been that morning, but now it was too low-tide, and they'd really scored it. They were boasting so blissfully, it made Mike and I nauseous. So I got my movie camera, he jumped on his board, and we paddled about a mile down the coast to Padang. It's probably the closest thing to Pipeline I've ever witnessed, and it's nasty. It breaks right in front of a cliff and these huge boulders, and at low tide, the waves come in and just become mutations, trying to destroy themselves on the shallow reef. We wound up riding all day by ourselves. I was just having fun, but Mike was riding the biggest waves, just re-defining the limits of what can be done out there. We hiked back up the coast, and for the rest of the day we were reverberating, just bouncing off the walls. We couldn't believe what we had seen and done."

• At a spot near Kona, on the Big Island, Stewart and some friends arrived at a remote surfing break just before dark. The place is known for its black-sand beach, waves Stewart calls "heaving, horizontal slabs". . . and sharks. "We stood there about 30 minutes, scared to go in, but we finally did," Stewart says. "Every now and then, boils of water would surge up for no apparent reason, and moments of terror would hit you like a bullet." But they rode the place at night, anyway.

• In early December, 1988, Stewart was seen coming out of a treacherous Pipeline cavern, then getting tubed and re-appearing *twice* more before blasting out, launching into a spectacular aerial 360, and making it. "It may well be the most advanced 10 seconds of surfing ever seen, anywhere," wrote *Surfer*.

• While the 1990 Eddie Aikau contest was being held in 20-25-foot surf at Waimea Bay, Stewart drove down to Laniakea to check out the cloudbreak known as Himalayas, about three-quarters of a mile out. He studied the place, weighed the emotions of fear and confidence, and finally said, "I'm on it." In the company of just two other surfers, Mike had an unbelievable session. "It was awesome, like 25-foot G-Land," he said. "It was wild. The wind was blowing so hard out there, you could hardly get into the wave. I saw one of those guys get lifted into the air on takeoff and he was just suspended there, like he was flying. Then he got blown right out the back. It was scary; the whole ocean would just *surge* up. It was probably the biggest surf I've ever been in. I'm *there* now, every time it's big."

Just who the heck is this guy, anyway? And where on earth did he come from?

That's what a lot of bodyboarders were asking in 1982, when Stewart entered the Sandy Beach contest on Oahu's east side. He was 18, and ripping, and it was his very first contest, and he had a Morey Boogie board. "Keith and I and Pat Caldwell had one, but nobody else in the world," Severson recalled. "Or so we thought. That was a weird introduction. Mike was like a total mystery."

He had grown up in Nuuanu, Oahu, with a pretty good background in adventure. His mother, JoAnn, was relentlessly active as a licensed pilot, ocean swimmer, scuba diver, golfer and tennis player. "My dad pretty much charged, too," Mike says. "He was brought up like I was: *haole*, Caucasian-born and raised in Hawaii, which is pretty tough."

Bob and JoAnn split up, for good, when Mike was just four years old. "I just remember him as a real 'edgy' guy. He liked to be on the edge of things. He rode bikes, got into drag racing. He was always downstairs, taking apart a Chevy and rebuilding it. He's in California now, and still a total kid. He likes to drag-race at stoplights, stuff like that. He's like, 'Oh, yeah, I did a great job on a Ferrari the other day.' Pretty classic. He really doesn't know me at all. But he's the first one who took me surfing."

Mike wasn't a very big kid. In fact, JoAnn thought he was going to be a midget. "He didn't grow up until he was 18," she says. "They used to beat up the *haoles* every Friday in Honolulu. Out at Sandy Beach they did that, too; usually guys on drugs. You fought back or you'd get in worse trouble. They'd come after you later. Mike never went looking, but he would never back down."

"People here are a lot more humble," Mike says. "They're living on a lot more primitive level, and the laws of the jungle apply here more. That might sound kind of far-fetched, but it's true. If you get out of line, start being cocky, they're not gonna tell you to shut up, they're gonna hit you [laughter]. I've been pretty feisty my whole life. I've had my teeth knocked in, I've been beat up thoroughly. I've been in fights that lasted almost an hour. Just beating the shit out of each other."

To this day, there's the slightest pidgin lilt to Mike's voice. "He can *really* speak pidgin when he wants to," says JoAnn. "I've listened to Mike and his friends sometimes, and they get into it where you can't understand a word. It really helps to do that if you're around local kids. Mike's got it down."

In 1975, JoAnn moved the family (Mike, then 12, and his older brother) to the Big Island. In a remarkable coincidence, one of their Kona neighbors happened to be Tom Morey, one of the true innovators of surf design and inventor of the first boogie board in 1971. Stewart was fairly interested in body-boarding, but when he met Morey, it became an obsession. "Tom took over as a father figure for me. I was 16, 17, just another kid at school, but once I got to Tom's I was like this mad scientist. Ideas would just flow, being with this guy. He had a sign: 'This Is Where The Impossible Becomes Possible.' At first he would only allow me downstairs. All the top-secret stuff was upstairs, the rest was rejects. That was fine with me; I would have paid him to work there."

Morey's hideout was a maze of swim fins, sketches, aerody-namic designs, experimental board shapes and beyond. "I took on Mike as a cleanup boy, but we wound up doing some interesting things," Morey said recently from his home in Winslow, Washington. "When it was his turn to talk, he usually had something to say. I took extra care with him, and he wound up dating my daughter, Melinda, for a while. He got to be recognized in the water before long. Unusual guy, Mike. He was always surfing these treacherous breaks with a lot of rocks, and nobody else around."

Stewart had no idea what people like Lindholm, Kaimi, Caldwell and Severson were doing on Oahu. He came up with spectacular maneuvers, like the aerial 360, completely on his own. "I always thought there was room to explore, and my imagination would just run wild. I remember having a dream that I was out surfing, and waves were coming in the size of valleys."

"Did you pull around and take off?" I asked.

"No [laughs]. Too weird."

He found the local drug scene a little too weird, as well. "I never did get into that. I tried it really early, like the fifth grade, and I felt like I was losing control of my body. I won't stand for that. There are some surfers who smoke it up before they go out there. Gives 'em the edge, where they'll be real carefree. I can't believe that. Much too dangerous. I can't even drink. I mean, I have one glass of wine and my whole night's shot."

By the time Stewart got to Sandy Beach for that first contest, he says, "I was totally ready. My experimentation was over. I didn't have a contest strategy, but I still finished third [Lindholm won it]." At his second contest, Mike met a lovely, Hawaiian-raised blond named Lisa Miller, a strong and healthy water girl, and they've been together ever since. Then came a third contest, and his first victory. Mike has a way of getting an awful lot done in a very short time.

JoAnn tried to get him a decent education, sending him first to a prep school in Santa Barbara, then to the University of Southern California, and despite his considerable talent for graphic design, it didn't work out. He was wearing his swim trunks to class, for crying out loud. "I finally said, 'Mike, if you drop out of school, you're going to have to support yourself,'" said JoAnn. "Because I wasn't going to do it."

Imagine her delight. Stewart earns a six-figure salary from

his contest winnings and endorsements, and there are no signs of his dominance ending any time soon. "He's just a couple of feet taller than everyone else," Morey says. "He's *there*, and the other guys are still being teenagers, clouded with second thoughts and peer pressure. Those guys pose as redwoods for a while, but they turn out to be oak trees. You only get a few redwoods, and Mike's one of 'em. It's in his heart—like somebody else is designed to sell tulips."

Tulips, eh?

"Tulips."

There's a perspective you may not have heard.

At the 1990 Morey contest, held in excellent 6-foot Pipeline, Stewart showed why he continues to stay on top. A lot of the competitors ripped, especially Severson, but Stewart's performance was just absurd. He wiped out on one wave, simply tumbled over the falls into oblivion, but beneath the surface he was still fighting—and he somehow reappeared in the whitewater, still riding, back from the dead. And while the other riders got deep in the barrel, they seemed intent only on coming out. Stewart had the knack of starting a new maneuver while he was still *way* back, hidden from view, so that when he did appear, he was already upside down in a full barrel roll. And making it, of course. His timing, confidence and weight distribution are unparalleled, and he has all the subtleties down, like finding those little windows and envelopes in a just-broken wave on his way out to the lineup. At times, he zips out there as if he were being towed by a jet ski.

It makes you wonder: Did Stewart ever consider stand-up surfing?

"It was never appealing to me," he says. "You've got this hard board, and you lug it to the beach, and the thing can really rack you. With bodyboarding, you get such a sense of speed when your face is that close to the water. All of your senses are involved. I don't think the surfers can imagine it.

"If I had my way, I'd be out at Pipeline, nowhere else. It's a pure, almost religious feeling, pulling into a giant cavern out there. You get deep beyond the point where you think you can come out, you're *long* gone from the beach…and you come out. It's *so wild,* man. You're totally in the jaws of death.

"I've had a lot of injuries out there—mostly to my ego [laughter]. I haven't been stuck in any holes [in the reef] or anything like that, but I've been pretty well drilled. I came into a sandy section one time, went in headfirst, and got buried all the way to my shoulders. If there'd been a rock there, I'd be history. I almost drowned another time when I got stuck on the inside, right in that zone where the rip is coming out like a river. Can't get in, can't get out. You're just stuck in the zone, getting pounded. That was scary."

It has reached the point where if a surfer sees Stewart coming, he's likely to back off—the ultimate tribute at Pipeline. "I'm not sure what they're thinking," he says. "Probably something like, 'Yeah, that guy's got a couple of bolts loose—let him go. He'll probably get reefed pretty soon, anyway.'"

Things are a little different at Sunset. According to Doerner, "Mike doesn't catch much respect there, because there's a lot of old-time big boarders that don't allow it. They're taking off way out there, ahead of everyone else, and they don't care who's in the way. A bodyboard is nothing to those guys."

Stewart ticked off Bradshaw once—in a big way. As Ken recalls it, "I don't like to hoot or shout when I'm taking off. I think it's really obnoxious. And Mike was out there hootin' and hollerin', like, 'My wave! Here I come!' Now, what gives him the right to this peak? Because he happened to paddle a little farther outside than me? I said, well, screw him, and all the people who act like him. I took off and I was flailing all over the wave, going [goofily] 'I'm a boogie, I'm a boogie.'"

We're talking about a couple of short-tempered guys here, and they both went off. They were ready to go. The fight never materialized, "and we've talked a lot since then," says Bradshaw. "I respect like hell what the guy does; he's amazing.

I was probably wrong, showing him disrespect. It seemed like fun at the time, but I guess I was out of line, a little bit."

"Yeah, I remember that," said Stewart. "He could have clobbered me, but I hate taking shit from surfers. You have to establish a presence out there. I've been taking that shit all my life, and I just won't take it any more."

If you want to talk real frustration, try Ben Severson. He sneaks in a contest victory occasionally but never, it seems, when it really matters. I caught up with Severson after one of his typically smoking sessions at Beach Park one day. "I think I've gotten too worked up to beat him," he said. "Sometimes the competitiveness drives me a little nuts. I'd like to see three or four more guys of our caliber competing. It would take the strain off between me and Mike." The two remain reasonably friendly, and their girlfriends, Lisa and Chris Ann Kim (a hot bodyboarder herself) get along well. But as Kim says, "Mike just doesn't socialize much any more. He's really secretive about everything. It seems like he just shows up, he surfs and he leaves. A lot of guys are intimidated by him. They don't even want to try."

And that's exactly what Mike is looking for. He trains and surfs alone, whenever possible, "because guys pick up on the new stuff I'm doing—particularly Ben. I know they have a lot of animosity toward me, and that's a bummer, because I grew up with these guys in the sport. But it's prohibitive to progress if you continue to be too amiable and sociable. I'd rather just exclude myself from the whole thing."

And like Tom Boyle says, he can be a little bit frightening. "The thing that always amazed me," said Boyle, "is that he'd be at USC two and a half months, come over straight from his final exams, paddle out into 12-foot Pipeline, and look like he never left. Everybody's saying, 'Oh, he's really white [no tan], he's been staying up late, he won't surf that well.' But he's got this drive in him, that he simply *can't* finish second, and it's scary because no one with all 52 cards in the deck would attempt the things he does on a regular basis. I mean, hey, I want to win the contest, too, but I enjoy being able to walk.

"It's like, some people are deep thinkers and some are not," Boyle says. "Mike definitely is, and unfortunately in sports, a lot of deep thinkers will think things over *too* much and psych themselves out. But Mike, somehow, is able to give himself momentary lobotomies [laughter], just pull off things that would make a paraplegic out of you or me.

"If you've ever been out at Pipeline [Boyle has ridden the place at considerable size], you know your instincts tell you to get the hell out of there. Mike is just the opposite. When he takes off…I don't know, you can just feel excitement running through your body, like something incredible is about to happen. Time after time. And you wonder, after Bjorn Borg wins five Wimbledons, after Robbie Naish is world champion nine years in a row, when do you stop getting interested in the next contest?"

How about it, Mike?

"There's always something to keep me going," he said. "Like right now, I'm looking forward to competing against Kainoa McGee. I can pick up certain vibes and attitudes at an event, and he pretty much thinks he's gonna win."

He paused, then unleashed a huge smile that explained everything.

But doesn't it get a little tiresome, just blowing everyone out of the water?

"It's kind of anticlimactic in a way," he said. "But [cheerily]…tough shit, man. I'm gonna keep going."

He will, too. He says he wants to ride maxed-out Waimea, and Kaena Point, and some of those other distant reefs where the swells hit 30 feet-plus and the winds howl so savagely it's a feat just to drop in, and he'll probably do all of that, too. Without bothering to bring any friends or photographers along. If you're out there thinking you can take Mike Stewart's place in the surfing hierarchy, remember, there's always time to find some other line of work.

Little Bits of History

December is often the best month for big, perfect surf on the North Shore, and it's always the most hectic. The onslaught of visiting surfers and ASP pros reaches its height in December, creating horrendous crowds, frayed emotions and a tragic absence of the *aloha* spirit.

It's amazing, though, how Pipeline puts all that madness to shame.

For two straight years, the most challenging day of the Pipeline Masters waiting period occurred when the contest was postponed. I was on the beach for both of those days, and they rank among the most memorable I've seen.

In 1988, contest organizers awoke to a gloomy, 12-15-foot day with glassy conditions but only a few makeable waves. Randy Rarick called off the main event without hesitation, saying, "It's just too dangerous. There's a time when you have to back off in the interest of safety." So here you had Pipeline, a little hairy but uncrowded, and you'd think this gathering of superstars might jump on the place for some much-needed practice. You'd be dead wrong. They wanted *no* part of it. Without the lure of prize money or the crowd's applause, they fled like thieves.

Nobody was blaming them—and yet, a few had their own ideas. As the day unfolded, it became apparent that Tom Curren, Tom Carroll, Mitch Thorson and Martin Potter, among others, were the genuinely committed surfers in the group—the ones who truly wanted Pipeline in a life-and-death situation. The session began in the early morning when Curren, Thorson and Tim Fretz (the noted hellman who would die of an apparent suicide within months) paddled out. They were later joined by Carroll, Potter, Mickey Neilsen, Pierre Tostee and bodyboarder Mike Stewart, who enhanced his reputation by sitting farther out *and* farther over (toward Off the Wall) than anyone.

It would be impossible to describe the caliber of surfing by Curren and Carroll that day. It went right off the scale. Although the cloudy, glassy day had a California look, it was savage, second-reef Pipeline, with an ominous north hook shutting down nearly everything inside. Curren's backside surfing was a masterpiece of grace, courage and wave knowledge, while Carroll—pioneering the helmet now worn by many Australians at Pipe—emerged from one frightening situation after another. Tostee got the tube of the day, placing himself inside a ridiculously large barrel and *not* coming out.

To top it off, Herbie Fletcher put on a heady display of jet-ski riding. It should be noted that jet skis are illegal, by city and county ordinance, in all North Shore surf outside the Haleiwa harbor. But the law is a bit difficult to enforce, especially when someone like Fletcher, Brian Surrat, Randy Laine, Brian Keaulana or Tony (Squiddy) Sanchez is at the helm. These guys know what they're doing. Nobody else would even *think* of hauling those machines out in big surf.

Fletcher, a hard-core Pipeline surfer since the late '60s, danced around three-story collapsing sections like a guy playing with his kids on the living-room floor. He even towed Carroll and Potter into the lineup from beyond the third reef, which seemed in questionable taste until Potter, after S-turning on his own through previously uncharted waters, got massively tubed and came out. The sun never appeared that day, and only a few people stuck around to watch. But it was vintage North Shore: apparently unsurfable conditions being ridden—expertly.

Switch now to the 1989 Pipe Masters, and a dark, rainy December morning with four days left in the waiting period. Again, the trials had been completed. Again, Rarick was waiting for a pristine day. And again the swell came up titanic and dangerous, with too much of a northerly direction, and the event was postponed.

Who would challenge it this time? Not surprisingly, most of the contest entrants were history. But another riveting session developed when Curren, Carroll, Cheyne Horan, Brad Gerlach, local standout Kolohe Blomfield and the incomparable Gerry Lopez went out. In this day of shameless self-promotion and multi-colored equipment, Lopez was a glorious sight with his white trunks and clear-deck board. He was simply the master in his element. No sponsors required.

Blomfield must have had 15 rides, identical in their precision. Curren again met the task, dropping into cavernous Backdoor rights and not only making them, but avoiding the hell of being caught inside. Going left, his smooth bottom turns and powerful off-the-lips conjured up memories of Hawk, Owl, Rabbit, Shaun...the very best backside invaders from other shores. If anyone tells you Curren can't surf big Hawaii, take pity on the poor soul and pray that he'll come to his senses.

The rain began falling, relentlessly. On the beach with my bodyboarding partner Chris Tellis and his friend Stewart Brand, founder of *The Whole Earth Catalog,* we had to wonder what we were doing. We'd been watching for an hour, we had seen enough, and we were thoroughly soaked.

The reason was simple: Lopez. He was still out. You simply don't turn your back on that kind of theater (although, looking around us, we realized we were alone). Fittingly—and remarkably, for a man pushing 40—Lopez took a death-defying drop, disappeared behind the curtain and coolly glided onto the shoulder. The wave of the day.

As Lopez got out of the water, he noticed these rain-drenched fools just standing there, watching him. "Not a fit night out for man nor beast," he announced, chuckling as he ran by.

* * *

February 3, 1989: I've taken a house right on Sunset Beach, looking directly into the lineup. Sometimes from the parking lot, where most people check the break, Sunset doesn't look that heavy. From my spot, it was truly intimidating. From this angle you see the proper perspective—swells arriving from all directions, the impact of a thundering lip on the inside reef, and a pretty good sense of what it's like to be caught inside. There were days when I'd take a long look, start to get waxed up, and suddenly one of those preposterous sets would come in, just cleaning up the whole crowd. And I'd suddenly think, "Gee—wonder if there's a ballgame on?"

On one particular afternoon, it was coming in at 10-15 feet against a nasty sideshore wind. The place was unruly, just a mess, under constantly threatening skies. In the late afternoon I spotted two surfers out there, challenging the place head-on. They were doing well, riding with confidence on the few manageable waves that came through. Then one of them got horribly caught inside. His board shot crazily into the air and came loose—a broken leash. The set was just beginning, and I didn't see his head for several minutes. Finally there he was, in the right spot, letting the whitewater thrash him in. I retrieved his board and hung around the shoreline, hoping to catch a glimpse of this person who was, essentially, surfing Victory at Sea alone.

It was Cheyne Horan. Thumbs-up, smiling, downright cheery. Looked like he'd never been better. When I mentioned this incident to Trevor Sifton, he didn't seem at all surprised. "Oh, Cheyne does that all the time," said Sifton. "He's totally fried."

* * *

110

February 14, 1974: the rookie season. I'd been watching Pipeline for nearly four weeks, and while I was flat-out petrified of big Sunset and Waimea, Pipe had sort of a haunting appeal. I couldn't go home without having *some* sort of experience out there. It was a postcard-perfect day, with a pure west swell that made it relatively easy to get out: hit the water, drift north with the speeding current, ease through the sandbar between explosions, then paddle toward the lineup—as close as you dare.

It was a solid 10-12 feet. The drops were 20 if they were an inch. Gerry Lopez, Rory Russell and Mike Armstrong were dominating the lineup, and as I watched this time-honored scene unfold, I knew I'd never be one of those guys sitting on or behind the peak. This was the big leagues. I made this entry in my '74 journal:

"The session was unbelievable. It had me in a daze until sunset, and for weeks afterward. The things I saw have to come first: Lopez, taking off at the most critical spot, handling the drop with incredible grace, making nearly all of his treks into the unknown. Armstrong just as solid, which is scary. Rory had a horrible day, with two very bad wipeouts that I saw. On the first one he didn't come up. I was right there; the man did not come up. I heard later he'd been trapped inside a cave— probably the ultimate North Shore horror story—and was down there longer than he'd care to remember. Then, on his next wave, he got a bit too casual and got slammed down by the head. Of course, he was *way* back there to begin with; that's the whole story. The power, horror and perfection of Pipeline is hard to grasp as being real."

I didn't have a leash then. [In fact, I didn't wear one until I was 38; clinging to some traditionalist nonsense, I was an annual leader in swims to the beach.] One set came in with kind of a north bend, and as I scratched over it, the wave simply ripped the board out of my hands and delivered it down around Beach Park. Later, a harmless-looking little right came in. Hey, this is my chance, I thought. The ride was short and pointless, and as I pulled out... Oh, *no*. A monster set was approaching.

I sat there in the impact zone, waiting for this new version of hell, and wow, did this wave deliver. I couldn't have been in more than eight feet of water, but I wound up in total desperation, clawing for the surface on what I felt were the final breaths of my life. Fortunately, the washing machine spat me out of range for the next wave. I'm not sure I would have survived it.

My friend Jack Pritchett and I used to describe bad wipeouts as "eating chota." Before that session was through, I lurched into a few shoulder takeoffs, elevator-style drops I'd never seen before, and ate serious chota. Just free-falling, into the air and out of the picture. Those early days on the North Shore taught me a lifetime's worth of lessons—mainly this: You should never go out, anywhere, unless you're ready to attack the biggest waves and have fun doing it. Anyone else is a fraud out there, and should be removed by the Bureau of Taste.

* * *

February 1989: Dane Kealoha paddled out at Pupukea one sunny afternoon and staged a performance that must have been typical for him, but was mind-blowing for the occasional visitor. His moves seemed orchestrated, yet spontaneous, the way he accentuated every takeoff, bottom turn or lip slam with a facial expression or an artistic wave of the hand. Even during the lulls, he was distinctive. You've seen surfers try to stand on their boards in quiet water; they teeter and jerk around, and finally crash. Dane did this, in a crouch, for many seconds without a twitch. Then he fully stood up to check a set coming through, his board holding firm underneath him all the while. A bit later, I saw him sitting on his butt, legs crossed in a yoga position, steadfastly paddling by. Quite the fine thing.

* * *

North Shore myths:

1. *You can't get waves.* Gracious, can you get them. They're everywhere, and they will reduce you to nothing. You're lucky if the surf goes *down.*

2. *You'll get long, perfect rides.* Not likely. You'd be surprised. Give yourself at least six weeks if you want a guarantee. Closeouts, less-than-ideal winds and generally unnerving conditions are the norm. One thing for certain, though: you'll get the *takeoffs* of your life.

* * *

January and February, 1976: In terms of spectator viewing, nothing will ever match this. Day after day, I watched Shaun Tomson, Rabbit Bartholomew, Peter Townend, Ian Cairns, Michael Tomson, Mark Warren and Mark Richards ripping Pipeline and Off the Wall. I shot miles of Super-8 film, usually not far from Bill Delaney, who turned his footage into the best surfing film of the last 20 years (*Free Ride*). I remember turning off my camera, twice, during Shaun Tomson tube rides, because he was long gone inside the barrel—yet he made it out. Rabbit surfed with incredibly dramatic flair, one of the all-time stylists, and his backside approach to Pipeline often took on the look of a death wish.

There were other moments, too. Wayne Lynch, probably the surfer I'd admired most over the years, appeared at Pipeline around 11 one morning. He took one wave, pulled out early, then got sucked over the falls of the second wave. He came to the beach, bleeding profusely from the jaw, and a very concerned-looking Townend helped him to the hospital. Later that day, I asked Townend if Lynch was OK. "Yeah, he said. "A bit delirious...."

Some journal entries:

January 28: "Each day seems to bring more waves, more sun, and a little more history. You try to leave, pull yourself away from it, but you just can't walk away from this performance...There were no other casualties in the water, as far as

113

I could see, and that made Lynch's injury seem all the more haunting. I woke up in the middle of the night, completely psyched out after some kind of caught-inside nightmare, and the sound of waves crashing outside made it tough to get back to sleep. I keep having to win my own confidence back."

February 1: "Hello, National Weather Service? What's that, another 12-foot swell? Nutty."

February 3: "Now I know why I've been bored at nights. I don't have a car, a phone, a clock, a TV or a human."

February 5: "The spell is broken. There was solid, Hawaiian-style six-foot surf and bigger for 22 straight days."

February 12: "Some off-the-wall flashes: Jeff Crawford at Pipeline, so far over, so precise...Gas Chambers, glassy and looming...Rory Russell, just hanging around and riding Pipe ...Rabbit's vertical slams—can't be done any better...Shaun's instinctive, explosive frontside cutbacks; possibly the hottest surfing ever seen...The style of Richards; an innovation. Who else has a body so located?...Pleasant tales of BK, the king of Sunset for all time...Lopez, who lives on Maui, comes over and leaves no doubt. Who could possibly drop in on Lopez?... The bottom. Good lord, the bottom."

As the years passed, it struck me that the winter of 1975-76 was not only historic, but singular in its performance level. Ten, fifteen years later, we *still* haven't seen a run of surfing like that. "It's really true," Bernie Baker confirmed. "Except for a couple of maneuvers that almost came out of the skateboard world, like aerials and floaters, everything's held up pretty well. While much of surfing has changed, a lot of it has not."

* * *

Baker is always a pure source—if you can find him. Photographer, judge, contest organizer, *Surfer* Magazine editor, Sunset regular...the man is busy all day, every day. Amazingly, I caught up with him for a couple of hours one night. He talked about the lords of his favorite break:

114

"I remember the first time I saw Ian Cairns surf Sunset. Up until that time, nobody—but nobody—ever touched Jeff Hakman. Just couldn't be done. The roster will show you how many awards that man has won. But one afternoon, I remember looking out and seeing this guy make it from the outside portion of the reef, on a big northwest swell, and come across the flat spot. He entered the main peak, the primary lineup, from 50 yards back, threw his board straight up into the lip, and came straight back down to the peak—exactly where most guys paddle for the wave initially. The man had already gone 120 yards. Then he'd crank off a bottom turn, single fin, and just *fly*—right across the inside wall. I watched him do this all afternoon. We were spellbound. In his professional years, he was one of the very best who ever came to Hawaii.

"Barry Kanaiaupuni, without a doubt, was the most *radical* surfer out there. Even after he was semi-retired, you just didn't see guys pulling off what he did in his prime. He was the only guy who truly danced in the water. Everyone else surfed. He danced. He would rock his board from side to side, going down on the takeoff. You don't see guys doing that on Thrusters today. It would loosen up the board, and make it very free for the bottom turn. He'd actually kick-stall at the top, and *really* let it get steep, and *then* fall down the face. He'd let the lip fall down on top of him—intentionally—and keep going. You look at the old Hal Jepsen films; nobody's surfing in any shape or fashion today that will take anything away from what he did."

Baker also told the story of his encounter with Al Unser, one of the all-time greats of race-car driving, at Honolulu International Airport. "Myself, Leonard Brady, Dane Kealoha and a couple of other guys were coming back from an awards banquet in California, and we saw Al Unser on the shuttle from the car-rental agency. I mean, this guy goes 204 mph around the track. I went up to him and said, 'I realize you're Al Unser. Can I have your autograph?' He says, 'Aw, hell, yeah —what are you boys doin', anyways?' I told him we were surfers from Hawaii. 'Aw, hell, I seen that on TV,' he says. And I showed him this trophy that Dane had won, which happened to be a framed photo of Dane cranking a big backside bottom turn at Pipe. Al Unser looked at it, just stared at the thing for about ten seconds, and finally said, 'God damn. No way in *hell* you'd catch me in somethin' like that.'"

* * *

A word about kneeboarding: I've never had the pleasure of watching Ray Pino, the great Maui rider, or some of the Wedge boys, like Steve Lis and Ron Romanosky, in North Shore surf. But I can't imagine anyone matching the performance of Rex Huffman at Pipeline in the mid-'70s. As the years went on, Huffman suffered a series of major injuries that severely curtailed his riding. On one harrowing afternoon at Big Rock, his home break in Southern California, Huffman broke his kneecap and severed some of the muscles and tendons underneath it. But he kept coming back. They say he never knew the meaning of fear, and in February of '74, I saw him attack 12-foot Pipeline in a phenomenal, week-long display of guts and wave positioning. As far as I'm concerned, his screaming bottom turns, tube riding and flat-out speed set the standards in this sport for all time, and this guy didn't just ride Pipeline. He stuck his *face* in it. Huffman wound up winning a North Shore Expressive contest at Pipe in '77 (with Pino third), which was appropriate, because it lent an official stamp of credibility to his act. The man should know that he's remembered.

* * *

You never know who you'll run into around here. One afternoon, venturing into the closely guarded waters of Backyards, I saw Nat Young paddling by. It was early 1989, and he had recently turned 41. Historically, Nat might go down as the No. 1 surfer in all of Australia—and here he was, enjoying the North Shore for the 26th consecutive year. "Even if it's just

116

one or two weeks, I love coming over," he said. "You see that structure up on the hill there?" He pointed to a large cement bunker, a lonely remnant from World War II. "In 1969, Mike Tabeling and I put up some mosquito netting and spent three months in there. Back then it was just Haleiwa, Sunset and Waimea, with 15 or 20 other guys. We were never pushed to other spots."

That certainly isn't the case now. In February of '90, I was enjoying the rare pleasure of bodysurfing near Log Cabins with Mark Cunningham when I noticed a lone surfer in the water. It was a beautiful day, but the shorebreak surf couldn't have been more than two feet. "What's that guy doing?" I asked Cunningham. "Isn't that kind of a bad look?"

Not really—not when it's Wayne Lynch.

Here's a guy who will drive 500 miles across Australia, hike another five miles, climb uneasily down sheer-cliff terrain, then leap into the ocean off some pile of rocks to ride stormy, 18-foot surf by himself. A true-to-life legend in every sense of the word. I know I've never been the same since watching Lynch surf La Barre (France) in Paul Witzig's film, *Evolution*, in the late '60s. And here was Lynch, riding the most insignificant waves you'll ever see during a North Shore winter.

He and Cunningham enjoyed a warm greeting. "I checked the whole coast," Lynch told him, "and this is the only place that's uncrowded."

* * *

No matter how many times I see Herbie Fletcher's jet-ski ride at 25-foot Waimea (featured in the "Wave Warriors II" video), I find myself in complete disbelief. He made the drop but was slowed by chop, and in the jet-skier's ultimate nightmare, the wave caught up with him. He rode that thing at least 50 yards with nothing more than a two-handed grip, while the rest of his body flailed and lurched in the whitewater. He would disappear for several seconds at a time, then come back into view, still hanging on for dear life. He wound up riding it all the way to the beach, where he surged to a stop and climbed off, stunned and wobbly-legged.

"It was a big, closeout wave," he told me on the beach at Pipeline a year later. "I could see the set coming two miles away at Log Cabins. It was about the biggest I'd ever seen. I just said, 'Well, this is what I came here for.' I let the first two go by, then jumped on the third, which usually is the biggest. It was like going 45 miles an hour on a 50-foot wall of water, like being on the freeway in the tube. The Blue Highway. I hit a big chop the size of a Volkswagen, and from that point on I just couldn't plant my feet. I was just hitting bumps and sucking air. I remember surfing 15-foot Pipeline in the dark back in '68, and I always felt that was the scariest situation I'd been in. But this was the heaviest thing ever."

* * *

The sign of a real water man: On December 13, 1989, in the middle of the Pipeline Masters waiting period, Tom Carroll and some Australian friends went bodysurfing in overcast, onshore, six-foot, sucking-out conditions at a spot known as Insanity Sandspit. Just about everyone I've talked to agrees that this is *the* heavy shorebreak in Hawaii, and it has claimed dozens of lives. If you see someone heading out there in big surf, he's either (a) a king-hell bodysurfer or (b) in tremendous trouble. But there was Carroll, getting a good 10-15 waves for fun, just laughing away, and he wasn't even wearing fins. Good stuff.

* * *

North Shore lifeguard Rick Williams moved to the North Shore from Hermosa Beach in 1974, when he was just 15. He and Doug Brown came over together, each graduating from Waialua High, and while Brown had a passion for insanity—riding Pipeline just as big and frightening as it got—Rick preferred the longer, more cerebral rides at Sunset and Haleiwa. He tells a couple of Haleiwa stories:

"When I was 18, I paddled out at 12-plus Haleiwa and immediately realized it was too much. It was so big, I was scared; I knew right off the bat I shouldn't be out there. It was kind of neat, though — there were about 20 guys out, guys that could really handle it: James Jones, Ben Aipa, Larry Bertleman, Charlie Smith. Just being out there, and watching them take off on these waves, was pretty heavy. It was like quadruple overhead. I got an inside wave that was at least 10 feet, got back to the beach and kissed the sand. You learn from that. You find out exactly what your limits are, and how big your balls are.

"It's different now, but in some ways it really isn't. Just the other day [February of '89] it was raining real hard, and they told a bunch of us [lifeguards] to sit inside the surf center at Haleiwa until the weather broke. So we got down there, and the wind was blowing straight offshore. Pouring rain and about 3 feet, but the conditions were unreal. We paddled out, Darrick and I and a few other 'guards, waiting for the regular crew to show up, but they never did. Pretty soon, maybe 45 minutes later, it's coming up—6 feet, then 8 feet. It ended up being six lifeguards and just a couple of others. I felt like a little kid that day; we were all out there ripping, jumping around on the beach, but more than that, we were just stoked. Wave after wave. Having the *best* time. It's just reassuring to know you can still get that. As long as it still happens, I'll keep playin'."

Stepping Out

A most unusual and special event occurred in the middle of February, 1990. For the first time ever, a group of women had Pipeline all to themselves.

It was the first annual Women's Bodyboarding World Championship, organized by big-wave Hawaiian rider Carol Philips, and it was something to see. The waves peaked at about 3-5 feet, which was a shame, because Philips and a formidable crew of Brazilian riders were eminently ready for *real* Pipeline. But it was a gorgeous day, a jewel in an otherwise bleak waiting period, and one got the feeling that bodyboarding is the future of women's surfing on the North Shore.

The sport is growing fast. A distinct rivalry is developing between the Brazilians—some 20 strong each winter—and the Hawaiians, led by Philips, Chris Ann Kim and Shawnee Oide. It shouldn't be long before Japan, Australia and California enter the picture. The mixture of ability, courage, aesthetic beauty and femininity reaches a rare level in bodyboarding— perhaps more so than in any other women's sport—and it quickly became evident that the Pipeline contest, in its own way, was just as appealing as a men's event.

The stand-up scene, meanwhile, seems to be stuck in neutral. Maybe even taking a few steps backward.

Back in the '70s and early '80s, the women had a treasured niche. Margo Oberg, Lynne Boyer and several others surfed good-sized North Shore waves with supreme confidence, and Hawaii was the focus of the women's surfing world. Today, you'll hear an occasional mention of Lisa Andersen, Jodie Cooper, Karen Gallagher or Betty Depolito ripping the North Shore waves, but it's little more than a casual footnote. To hear some tell it, the women's tour is in danger of folding due to lack of interest.

"When the pro tour was restructured in '83, it completely killed women's surfing," says Randy Rarick, who ran the 1988 and '89 women's events on the North Shore. "The emphasis shifted from Hawaii to Australia, and when you took the Hawaiians away, it came down to who was keen enough to be a small-wave rider. So you had the emergence of Frieda Zamba, Kim Mearig, Wendy Botha…you know, hey, they're great in little waves, but they don't do shit over here.

"In terms of impact, the stuff Margo, Lynne and Jericho [Poppler] did eight years ago was *way* better than today. The equipment is better now, and I guess technically, you'd have to say that Jodie Cooper's surfing at Sunset is better. But it isn't more advanced. Not in relation to what the women were doing back then, on inferior equipment.

"The way it stands now, the women need a major injection of Hawaiian sponsorship and support," Rarick said. "Otherwise, they should just towel the whole thing. I mean, let's be real. That's really where it's at. If you had more events here in Hawaii, and you encouraged a new group of girls to really charge it, great. But in its present structure, they're a sideshow to the men, and that's being benevolent. The event here at Sunset was the most exciting they had all year, but you watch 'em at any other spot, like [cringing] Huntington Beach, and it's just terrible. It's embarrassing."

Depolito thinks the women are doing just fine, actually, and she sees a big future for people like Cooper, Andersen and Pauline Menczer of Australia. But she agrees with Rarick to an extent. "Those really were the good old days," said Depolito, who came to the North Shore from Encinitas in '79. "It was big-wave surfing, and the ASP catered to it. The whole circuit was different. I've surfed Waimea around 15-18 feet, and I've been out in 10-foot Pipe, and hey—I do OK. I think women should be forced to push themselves into bigger surf. I say, 'Why don't you guys have a contest at Pipeline, maybe 6-8 feet?' They're not into it. Most of 'em won't do it.

"But it's hard, you know? Sure, you can say women don't ride big waves, but there are a lot of factors involved," Depolito said. "We've got a lot of pressure: the femininity thing, the physical thing, just the aggressiveness of it all. It's kind of a psych-out for a lot of the women. When a man gets all 'aggro' out there, it's OK. With a woman, it's like all of a sudden you're a dyke, or something. I mean, these are the perceptions we're dealing with.

"It's just really hard—mentally and physically. Jodie can definitely surf 10-foot Sunset, but I can't talk her into going out at Waimea. Most of these girls just figure, why even bother? Maybe they're smarter than I am; maybe they just show good sense. I guess there's a lot of things you can do in life where you don't have take such punishment. And remember, also, you've got to put in *time* to ride these waves. There just aren't many women who choose to live on the North Shore and put up with a lineup full of guys. Boy, I sure had fun, though [laughter]."

It's entirely possible that the new generation of Hawaiian women will be bodyboarding, not surfing. They certainly have the role models: Philips, who turned that Pipeline contest into reality through sheer perseverance, and Phyllis Dameron, the only legitimate big-wave rider in the history of women's surfing.

Just to make sure, I asked some reliable sources about stand-up surfers in big waves. Such as:

Has a woman ever ridden 12-15-foot Pipeline?

Mark Cunningham: "Next question."

Has a woman ridden 20-foot Waimea?

Ken Bradshaw: "No, nothing beyond 12-15. Betty is the only woman who even has an inkling to ride Waimea."

How about 15-foot Sunset?

Bernie Baker: "Not to my recollection. We had Becky and Blanche Benson, Dale Dahling, Laura Blears from the Makaha side, but they never rode waves of that size. It just doesn't work. What's really funny—in a strange, demented sort of way —is that when Margo and Lynne Boyer semi-retired from serious surfing, the only woman riding big waves, consistently, was on a bodyboard. Phyllis Dameron."

And she goes *after* it. She's the lone wolf, a renegade, with no desire to enter a contest or even reel in a sponsor. It's all very simple for Phyllis: When Sunset gets big, she's on it. When Waimea pushes 20 feet, she's out there pushing her limits. "Phyllis was the first boogieboarder, man or woman, to really do something on the North Shore," said Baker. "She was out there, puttin' it on the line, before any of the names you're hearing now. She's a character, too."

I can attest first-hand that for a bodyboarder, getting "air" on the face of a wave isn't the most pleasant experience. The idea is to glide, not bounce. Yet, Dameron *thrives* on air. She insists on it. "I can't do that bellyspin, off-the-lip stuff at Sunset, because I've got to deal with surfboards," she says. "If you just stay in the wave on a bodyboard, you're too slow. It's just that simple. You've gotta skip. Not so much bounce, really, as skip. For me, that's the fun.

"You really get some mountainous chop at places like Sunset and Waimea, and you have to make that work for you," she says. "If you're skipping like a stone, you can land anywhere. And guys get intimidated by that. I'll go right over 'em, in the air if I have to, and it makes 'em nervous to see me flying around like that. The bigger the wave, the more you want to be airborne."

Now 35, a blend of Greek and German parentage, Dameron was born in Pasadena but has lived in Honolulu since her infancy. She got the usual training at Sandy Beach and Makapuu, and years of water time have given her the powerful build of a long-distance swimmer. Which is strange, because Phyllis insists she doesn't swim very well.

"Not at all," she says. "I don't feel like I'm good enough to swim in when it's 15 feet at Sunset. I'm just not. I'm out of there *real* fast. That's always in the back of my mind—how to swim in."

"She gets really scared when she loses her board," says Sunset regular Mike Latronic. "I remember one time it was really big and the rip was moving out, and she'd lost her board and one of her fins. She was just, 'Mikie! Mikie!' And I'm just a scraggly, 17-year-old kid on a 6-4, going, 'Uh-*huh?*' I'm trying to pawn her off to Richard Schmidt or somebody with a giant board. They finally called the helicopter and dragged her in eventually. That's Phyllis. She's a legend, and she's a menace."

"Hey, that was eight years ago," noted Latronic's female companion, coming to Phyllis' defense.

And Dameron has learned. Baker helped devise her a foolproof leash with a special cord fitting, "and I don't remember her having to swim in since then," he says. "I'm sure she's been down for the count, though. I'm sure she's sort of…seen God a couple of times."

"I could drown any year," she says. "I get tired out there; my judgment isn't always that good. But the older you get, the more you know when it's gonna turn on you. And if things get too scary, I don't wait for a set wave. I just take the whitewash in."

Surely, in such a male-dominated lineup, it must be difficult getting a wave at Sunset. "If I can't pass a guy in front of me, I won't go," she says. "If they're behind me, no problem. I can go off, let them have it, screw 'em over [laughter], it kind of depends who it is. That matters a lot. Who gets mad, who's got the muscle to back it up. I'm generally pretty courteous, but if I'm in position, I'll let 'em know. When I yell out, 'Hey! Hey!'…they don't know who's saying it. I almost sound like a man. I just yell, quick and sharp. If they think twice, then they're too late."

I asked Ken Bradshaw about Dameron. I figured they must have bumped heads over the last 10 or 12 years. "I think she's great," he said. "Hey, she's a big girl. She's 5-9, and *really* powerful. She puts down other girls, and I agree, most other girls are too frilly to go out there. But Phyllis can take it. She likes to bounce over people—set 'em up, then clear 'em. Pretty amazing. And she's out there because she loves it, which is the best thing of all. She's doing it for the right reasons."

In what kind of size? "Well, George Downing always says, if Phyllis is out, it's not big enough for a Waimea contest," said Bradshaw. "She really draws the line at 20 feet, because she doesn't have the ability to trim. At 15 feet you can ride like Phyllis and not get smashed. At 20 feet it lines up, and you've got to *hit* it."

Wave size on the North Shore is always debatable, but you'll find Dameron out there on days when most men don't even have their boards out. "I think I'm pretty different," she says. "Girls are girls, you know? They don't like the workout. I do. The Brazilian girls, I don't know, they just don't have it yet. They're still staying in the water, going slower. Carol Philips can do it. She likes Pipeline. She's pretty gutsy."

I knew Philips was a serious rider when I saw her at Pipeline one day, cascading down a face of at least 20 feet. She seems to be improving, too, because she was out at Waimea on the morning of the 1990 Eddie Aikau contest. "I took a gigantic free-fall that day," she said. "The wave was close to 20 feet, I'd say. It was pretty harrowing."

Her background, as it turns out, is even more interesting. "I grew up in a valley about two miles from any neighborhood, out in Kahalu," said Philips, 23, who also goes by the nickname Estelle. "It was kind of a hippie environment, really; we were home-schooled and vegetarian. We had no concept of social graces, acting cool, being 'on the scene,' that sort of thing. It was great, as far as I was concerned. My mother raised six kids and was really a wonderful influence. I grew up believing I could do what I wanted, that there were no limitations in being a woman.

"I was into kung fu and horseback riding back then, and I moved to the North Shore in '82 to ride horses. People can't believe this, but I had no idea what the North Shore meant. I'd done some bodysurfing on the East side and I was always good in the water, so when I saw Pipeline, I went out, just like that. Just blundered onto the scene. I didn't know who was who, or what photo was in which magazine—I didn't even know Pipeline was a famous wave."

Blissfully naive, Philips simply rode the North Shore as if she'd been there all her life. Just three years ago, she reckons, there were only four women bodyboarders taking on 10-foot surf: herself, Dameron ("my hero"), and a couple of Brazilian riders, France Hazar and Andrea Ferreira. Thanks to the Brazilians, who spend huge chunks of the winter in Hawaii, that number is growing. Philips and Chris Ann Kim co-founded the Hawaiian Association of Women Bodyboarders to foster some healthy competition, and it was through the HAWB that the Pipeline contest was born.

It almost didn't happen. On the day of the event, a group of Brazilians threatened to boycott the contest because the waves weren't big and they weren't getting enough prize money (only $600 to the winner). They backed off eventually but it was a poor-taste move, showing zero understanding of the event's historic significance. "Those girls should have been banned from contests for life," said one prominent male surfer, who happened to be on hand. "It was typical of the Brazilians' attitude over here—no manners whatsoever."

Philips, however, was in no position to take a stand. "The Brazilians represented 75 percent of the field," she said. "We probably couldn't have held the thing without them." So the show went on. The small conditions meant an early exit for some of the competitors, notably Philips, Hazar and hot Brazilian rider Cristina Munoz Carneiro. But there were some notable moments.

Liz Arlen, a 20-year-old rider from Maui, headed down to the beach on crutches. She was born with one leg. "A total inspiration," said Philips. "She's been in the water her entire life, and she's totally capable out there." Arlen surfed beautifully and finished eighth.

In a fine moment for Hawaii, Chris Ann Kim got the wave of the day. Chris had injured her jaw earlier in the day, but when a set wave came through, she launched into a huge aerial 360 and pulled it off, lifting her into a third-place finish. But the Brazilians were just too tough. Daniela Freitas, just 16, left a world of promise for years to come. Claudia Ferrari scored a second place, and there was no disputing the No. 1 trophy for Stephanie Pettersen, who staged a rhythmic, imaginative display of power surfing.

Afterward, Philips was already thinking about keeping the contest alive for future years. "I'll do my hardest not to let women get shafted like they do in stand-up surfing," she said. "It's not like we're so inferior. I mean, I've yet to see a man strong enough to hold up Waimea Bay and say, 'Stop. I am man.' I've had to deal with sexism, and I find it insulting.

"I think people are going to take notice of what we're doing. In bodyboarding you can retain your femininity, which I think most women prefer, and it's more of a family sport than board surfing. That's a real motivating factor. It's fun, it's easy to do, but it can be taken to a very high level."

The highest is yet to come.

Mike Foley, Surfer Magazine
Eddie Aikau

Steve Wilkings, Surfer Magazine
Eddie, "bully style" at the Bay

Vince Cavataio, Surfer Magazine
Clyde Aikau, in complete control of a heavy situation

Darrick Doerner at 10 — getting the feel of surfing in Malibu

Darrick took to the sport. Many contend that this wave (Waimea Bay, January 1988) was the largest ever ridden successfully.

Kimiro Kondo

Doerner at the Bay. He's been known to surf for hours without a cord or a mistake.

Vince Cavataio

Doerner: "Blue sky, green wave...perfect Hawaii."

Peter Simons, Surfer Magazine

Brock Little, just 22 years old, is making huge statements in big waves.

Vince Cavataio

Brock's classic tube ride during the Aikau contest

Warren Bolster

The 1986 Billabong signaled Brock's arrival at Waimea

Sequence by Tsuchiya, Surfin' Life Magazine

Brock didn't lose any points by wiping out on this wave. It was the "unridden realm," a legitimate 30-footer, and the mere attempt blew everyone's mind.

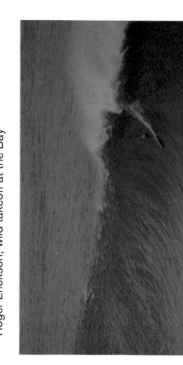

Gordinho

Roger Erickson, wild takeoff at the Bay

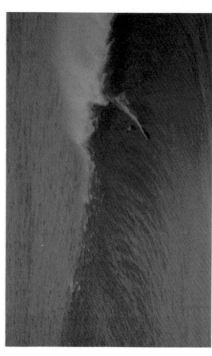

Bernie Baker

Keone Downing, winning the 1990 Aikau

Warren Bolster

"Blue corduroy" at Sunset Beach

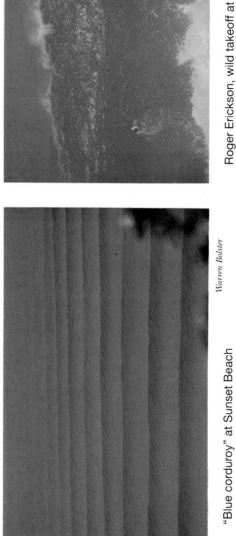

Warren Bolster

Owl Chapman, singular stylist

Don James

"Sometimes it's just too big."

Tsuchiya, Surfer Magazine

After Brock Little's epic tube ride at the Eddie Aikau contest, Tony Moniz said he "wanted to get one under my belt." He wasn't kidding.

Richard Schmidt at the Eddie: "Probably the heaviest wave of my life."

The Seasoned View

A discussion of big-wave surfing wouldn't be complete without a visit with Randy Rarick. Today's young surfers know him as the organizer of the Triple Crown pro events in Hawaii, but his credentials span the entire spectrum of the sport. Raised in Niu Valley, he started surfing in 1960. He became a hot competitor just as the short-board revolution began, and he was the Hawaii state champion before anyone had heard of professional contests. He surfed 20-foot Waimea at the age of 17, rode alongside the big-wave greats of the '60s and '70s, enjoyed a period as a successful shaper, and watched the sport evolve through Gerry Lopez, the Shaun Tomson-Mark Richards-Rabbit Bartholomew group, the Tommy Carroll-Tom Curren era, and now what he calls the "fourth generation."

At 40, Rarick has a firm grasp on the world surfing scene. He has visited 110 countries, surfing more than half of them. He's been to Japan some 30 times, Australia about 20; he has spent more than two years combined in Africa alone. "I've been to places nobody's ever surfed—before or since," he says. And he still surfs avidly—hitting the longboard circuit when he can, and catching all the best swells in his own back yard: Sunset Beach.

"I've seen 'em all come and go, and I'm still here," he says. "People go, 'God, Randy, will you ever grow up?'"

His answer, quite simply: "No."

Rarick says he might write his own book one day, and that's an intriguing prospect. For the moment, here are some of his thoughts on contemporary subjects:

Ken Bradshaw: "I've known Bradshaw since the day he came here. He was living in town, working as a bouncer at one of the local clubs there, and he came and bought a used board from me in '72. I didn't see him again for two years, because I sold my shop and traveled around the world. And when I came back, it was so funny, Bernie Baker had his house on Sunset back then. It used to be the 'hang.' If you were cool and you knew Bernie, you could park there. So I walk up to Bernie's early in the season, and Bradshaw comes up to me and says [intensely], 'It's *different* now, Rarick. You're not happening any more.' He gave me this full 'I'm hot shit' vibe, and I'm looking at him like, Bradshaw? Is that you? I sold this guy his first board over here. That was the beginning of his whole mission, when he was intent on being the king. I just said, 'Big deal. There's dozens of guys like you, pal.'

"But Kenny persevered. He kept plugging away, learned how to shape, kept riding waves, and that's *all* he did. So you knew he was going to be good. Trouble was, he was a jerk in those days. He used to drop in on everybody, just horribly — stuff I couldn't believe. He was like Ace Cool is now; people would hear Bradshaw's name and just roll their eyes. But it slowly changed. By the late '70s he'd put in enough time, and was getting good enough, so he commanded respect. I think 4-5 years ago is when Kenny really peaked. He's probably a better surfer now, but as far as his ascent up the ladder, around '83 was when he really made his mark. He and Booby [Jones] were the two best guys, and Foo was just starting to come on.

"It was really hard for Ken to accept the new generation. I think it *still* is for him. He's kind of in that mid-life crisis, where you realize, 'I've accomplished my task.' And once you do that, where do you go? It'll be interesting to see what happens. Booby Jones is a guy who's lost a little bit of his luster, but he's comfortable with his place in the scheme of things.

130

He's kind of like an aging football player who's still able to make the cut. Kenny is a mature big-wave rider who has reached his goal of achieving greatness. One of the best big-wave riders of his time. And now life goes on."

Mark Cunningham: "The thing that stands out about Mark, aside from his bodysurfing, is that he wasn't a jerk. He had enough *akamai* to know how to act around people. Whereas Bradshaw earned his respect, Cunningham *gained* it. And there's a difference. The classic example I always use is Mike Purpus. He had to earn his respect by being a good surfer, because he was just a jerk otherwise. There are certain guys that are just different enough that they gain it automatically."

Ricky Grigg: "Total inspiration to me. I mean, this guy's 52 years old, and he still surfs great—doesn't look any different than he did 20 years ago. He rides contemporary boards, and he's keen. You talk to Ricky and he's all excited. Whereas Peter Cole's like, 'I'm not gonna change. I'm stubborn. I'm doin' it my way. I'm wearing a white shirt.' And yet under that white shirt he's now wearing a rash guard [laughs], which he won't admit to. He won't wear a leash, either, and that's OK, because he's 57 years old and he's still out there in big waves. But Ricky's like, 'Hey, no way, give me a leash, give me a new board, I want to keep doing it.'"

Mark Foo: "I think Foo suffered from ego syndrome in the early stages of his career. He got a couple of magazine covers back in the '70s, people were super-jealous of him, and he was over-promoted before he really reached his full ability. So he had a heavy backlash—plus, he's a bit of an egotist. He sells himself, and people resent that. But I'll tell you, he does it well, and I admire him for it. I wish 50 more guys were acting like Foo. The sport would progress a lot more.

"Foo definitely could be a lot more humble at times, but in the last few years his ability has matched his sales job. Nobody disputes the fact that he rides Waimea really good. He kind of relies on that. I think he could be a bit more well-rounded. Like Brock [Little], for instance. He rides small waves good, he rips Sunset, and now he's an established big-wave rider. That's where Foo could have been, and missed out by devoting so much time to big waves. But that's what he wants. That's his tradeoff.

"I used to wonder with Mark: If there were no cameras, would he still be out there? Now I think he's transcended that. He does it because he likes it, more so than the publicity."

The Duke Contest: I especially wanted to get Rarick's view on this, because like most surfers over 35, I have fond memories of the Duke Kahanamoku Classic. It used to be televised by ABC's Wide World of Sports, and after suffering weeks of flat surf around Southern California, I'd build my entire day around watching this event. "If you ask me, it was the only true Hawaiian contest," says Bradshaw, "because it was a 24-man invitational, and they waited for the best *one* day at Sunset. Compared to the Duke, the entire ASP circuit is like a day at Ehukai Beach Park."

Billy Hamilton once wrote, "One of the most amazing things I've ever witnessed is the surf for the Duke meet. I've seen it flat for two weeks and jump to 15 feet the day of the contest. And I don't mean once or twice, but every year for 15 years now." The contest results bring back a flood of memories. Jeff Hakman, just 15 years old, won the inaugural Duke in 1965. The following year, Grigg left a Scripps Institute underwater experiment to hit Sunset and edge out Mike Doyle in "probably the cleanest conditions we ever had," said Rarick. In 1972, Hakman emerged from a Hall of Fame heat that included Barry Kanaiaupuni, Clyde Aikau, Reno Abellira and Hamilton—but it was Booby Jones winning it all on another classic day. Both of the Aikau brothers won the Duke, and when Bradshaw took the title in '83, he was so moved by the occasion he broke into tears. "I'm an emotional guy," he said. "I can still remember the cold winter day in '66, sitting back home in Texas, watching Ricky Grigg win the Duke. Then being in Hawaii, meeting all these people, and actually winning...I just couldn't handle it."

How could this contest possibly have died? Rarick, who helped support The Duke for years, was the right man to ask.

"Around 1970, the guy who was running the contest filed for bankruptcy, and he sold it for a token $1 to Henry Ayau, a longtime friend of the Kahanamoku family," said Rarick. "He ran it for 10 years purely on the rights-fee money paid by ABC. There wasn't much prize money, and nobody really cared; the prestige was more than enough. But in '82, ABC pulled out. That's when cable TV got big, and a lot of secondary sports were dropped by the networks. I took on the contest myself, and pretty much kept it alive in '83 and '84, but Henry wouldn't help me out. He wasn't prepared to sell the rights, and the thing just died—a death of no sponsorship and lack of management. Henry wouldn't hustle up a sponsor, but at the same time he wouldn't give up the rights. I actually went to Nadine Kahanamoku, the Duke's wife, to ask if I could take over the event. But she's in Henry's corner, because of the family association, and wouldn't go for it.

"This was one contest that really meant something. I surfed it in the early '70s and I still have my trophy. They gave one to each of the 24 competitors, and they were gold-plated Oscars [actually made by the same Hollywood company] with surfboards attached. Every surfer I know, if he kept one thing over the years, it was his Duke trophy. But it became a big financial headache for me. I lost $2500 out of my own pocket the last year, and then Michael Ho (who won it) complained that he didn't get enough prize money. He was so ungrateful, I couldn't believe it. That put me over the edge. We'd been running the contest on *kokua* and *ohana*, but when Michael pulled that stunt, I just said forget it. The spirit of the event had been lost for me.

"It could be revived. It could start up tomorrow," Rarick said. "Somebody would have to approach Henry and say, 'Here's $50,000. Give away $25,000, take $15,000 to run it, and stick the rest in your pocket. He's a super-nice guy. He's not into surfing, but he'd go for that.'"

So there you have it, all you rich sponsors with money to burn. Make out your check to Henry Ayau, and make it snappy, will you? The Duke has been dormant for much too long.

The Biggest Wave (Takeoff): "Greg Noll at Makaha, without question. That was killer, the swell of December '69. I was there. That was definitely the biggest wave I've ever seen a guy take off on. It happened on a Thursday, and I remember the swell coming up that Monday night. I was living with [Australian great] Keith Paull out on the point at Laniakea, and around 11 p.m., the Civil Defense guys came by saying, 'Get out of your houses. Evacuate. High surf coming.' I'm thinking, what's this shit? Give me a break. We just stayed put. But around 1 a.m. I was outside, sort of peering into that hazy mist you get when the surf really comes up. I watched a wave roll right up to the highway at Lani's. Then one rolled *over* the highway. Then I looked straight out, and there was this *huge* wall coming at me. I ran back into the yard, maybe 40-50 feet, and as the wave came up, it slammed into my hollow-tile wall and sent one of the bricks flying. It landed right at my feet. I'm going, 'Oh, my God!' I went into the house in a panic: 'Keith, wake up, we're gonna get washed away.' He just rolled over—you know, 'Go back to sleep.' We chanced it and hung in there.

"Turned out that was the peak of it. We got up at dawn the next morning, and it was chaos everywhere. Up at Ke Iki, four houses were just gone. One of them got completely washed across the highway to the mountain side. Cars were floating in like 10 feet of water, there were coconuts and sand everywhere. Sunset, Waimea, the whole North Shore was nothing but whitewater, for two miles out. I mean, it was like 50 feet. So we busted over to Makaha, and that was one of the best, biggest, cleanest days ever. A bunch of us were out: myself, Keith, Jimmy Blears, Rolf Aurness—he was living over there, couldn't have been more than 17—and the whole crew: Buzzy Trent, Greg Noll, Charlie Galento, Fred Hemmings, Bobby Cloutier, all the *heavy* big-wave riders. I was scared, but it was incredibly clean and glassy, just these 25-foot waves coming off the point. Open doors, all the way from the point across the bowl. There hasn't been a day like it since.

"Maybe you've seen the picture at Kua' Aina [the Haleiwa cafe]. Hemmings put that up there to embarrass me. He wrote in, 'Randy Rarick takes off in front of Fred Hemmings.' But I've got the next two shots *after* that. I made the wave and Fred got dusted. That's why I took off, because he was too far back, and I knew he wouldn't make it.

"The surf dropped a little bit the next day, but it came back up on Thursday—real stormy. The North Shore was totally blown out, and we all went back to Makaha and watched Greg go out there. It was unbelievable. As he was paddling into this wave, the bowl was already feathering. There was no way he could make it, and it was an *easy* 30 feet. We're all thinking, what's he doing? I guess Greg's whole deal was, he'd ridden Waimea as big as it gets, and this was gonna be his swan song. He got to the bottom and just jumped off. The thing unloaded on him. He just said, 'I'm gonna take off on this thing, the biggest ever, and it doesn't matter if I make it.' Nothing I've seen compares to that. Maybe one or two other guys paddled out that day, but nobody rode a wave. He was the only one who even tried."

The Biggest Wave (Ridden): "I've seen a lot of wild things. I was around when they filmed "Ride the Wild Surf," and that was giant. I saw Jock Sutherland and Jackie Eberly go *left* at Waimea, just a freak thing where they could get out the top real quick. I've seen Noll and Buzzy Trent, all those guys. I was paddling out in '67 during a big Waimea swell, and I've seen photos of Sammy Lee and Peter Cole on a solid 25-foot wave from that day. But they didn't make it. The biggest waves I've ever seen ridden, successfully, were by Darrick Doerner at Waimea. There were two of 'em—that Super Bowl Sunday [1988] and another wave about three years ago. He took off on these horrible, ugly monsters, with everybody on the beach

135

just going, 'Oh, no!' and he *rode* those things. He surfed 'em, made it out the other side.

"I think Darrick is the best surfer at Waimea Bay. I've been out there enough to make that statement. He doesn't have the flamboyance that some of the other guys do, but in the last three years, I watched him apply his knowledge to big waves, and he's out-done everybody else. You could say Brock's got more flash, or Bradshaw charges it more, and I've got tons of respect for guys like Owl, Booby, Bill Sickler and Gary Speece. But I've seen Darrick on waves pushing 30 feet and making it. That puts him in a different class. For sheer guts and going for it, he's the best guy out there."

The Hokule'a

"Eddie Would Go"

— North Shore decal

The field for the 1977 Duke Kahanamoku Classic read like a history of modern-day surfing. The Australians were there in full force: Mark Richards, Rabbit Bartholomew, Ian Cairns, Peter Townend, Mark Warren, Simon Anderson and one of Sunset's most distinctive masters, Terry Fitzgerald. Shaun Tomson and his cousin, Michael, were on hand. So were Bobby Owens, Dane Kealoha, Michael Ho, Larry Bertleman, Rory Russell, Buzzy Kerbox and longtime Haleiwa great Charlie Smith, to say nothing of big-wave standouts Keone Downing, Ken Bradshaw, Booby Jones and Clyde Aikau. And to top it off, there were three of Hawaii's greatest surfing legends: Reno Abellira, Gerry Lopez and Barry Kanaiaupuni.

The 24th man in that field, and the winner, was Eddie Aikau. Somehow, in typically classic Sunset Beach conditions, Eddie managed to outshine all of those men. At 32, he had reached the peak of his surfing greatness.

Just a few months later, he was dead. He died a hero's death, trying to save the lives of others. The memory of Eddie Aikau is just as fresh and alive today as it was after that fateful voyage of the *Hokule'a* on March 16, 1978. As far as the North Shore big-wave riders are concerned, his spirit will linger at Waimea Bay for all time.

"Eddie was more at one with himself than anyone I've known in my life," says Darrick Doerner, who joined Aikau on the North Shore lifeguarding crew in 1976. "We didn't hang around him, he didn't hang around us. He hung around himself.

"He didn't say much. The aura around him was intense. He'd go out in the water, and he wouldn't come in—not for food, for water, anything. Then he'd head in around dark, load up his boards on his car and split. That was his day at the beach. The partners, us guys, we'd bust our ass all day long. Whatever went out to sea, he would get. Other that that, we took care of the whole Bay. Awesome man. Lived an awesome life. Died in an awesome way."

The *Hokule'a* was a 60-foot, double-hull sailing canoe that would be making its second 3000-mile journey from Hawaii to Tahiti. Eddie was part of a select, all-Hawaiian crew and he had his 10-foot gun, hoping to do some surfing down there. The craft was about five hours out of Honolulu, nearing the midnight hour, when it was capsized by a huge swell in the Molokai Channel. A substantial storm was just beginning to take shape, and the crew held on grimly throughout the night, clinging to the hope that they would eventually be spotted by a Hawaiian commuter aircraft.

By morning, the situation had worsened. Southerly currents were driving the craft away from the islands, and there was pickup in both wind and swell. Aikau began wondering if he could paddle to the small island of Lanai, some 12 miles away, to get help. He would have a life vest, a rain slicker, a knife and a strobe light for assistance. The canoe captain, David Lyman, knew the odds would be stacked heavily against Eddie. He also knew Eddie was no ordinary man. As dusk approached, a decision would have to be made.

Eddie would go. Eddie *went*. Everyone aboard the *Hokule'a* lived to tell their story, having been spotted and rescued late that night. Eddie Aikau was never seen again.

"I went out to look for Eddie when he disappeared," said

oceanographer Ricky Grigg, who had shared Aikau's friend-ship on many big days at Waimea. "There were only two ships on the ocean—the Coast Guard and the University of Hawaii. I convinced the university to let me borrow their ship to go look for him. I've never been out in a storm like that. The wind was blowing so hard, the seas were so high, you couldn't even see another vessel. You could barely tell where the sea stopped and the air began; it was just a maelstrom of storm. The ship was rolling 45, 50 degrees on its side. We were on the edge of going over."

They searched from 7 a.m. until nightfall that day, with no sign of Eddie. "They said they found his surfboard," said Doerner. "But they didn't. They didn't find nothin', except the boat with everyone on it. Maybe he should have hung on. I sure would have.

"Put it this way: It's nighttime, with 20-to-30-foot white-caps," said Doerner. "You're not going to be able to hold a giant surfboard when you get hit by one of those. You just get broadsided. You get hit from all angles. The next thing you know you're a grain of sand, in a big ocean. If anyone could have survived that, Eddie could have. Just the attempt, though, the very *idea*...I had 'chicken skin' when I heard that."

An intensive search continued for a week after Eddie's disappearance, but nothing turned up. "As I look back on it, that was the only mistake Eddie ever made in the water," said Doerner. "Clyde doesn't talk about it much; it's been laid to rest. I remember Pops kept saying, 'My boy is out there. He's all right, he's all right. He's out there.' But Clyde wasn't saying that. He wears a lot of the pants in the family, and they finally called it off."

A memorial service was held about 10 days later at Waimea Bay—a sacred ritual at a sacred spot. For a just a moment, they say, it rained out of a clear-blue sky. "It was very quiet, with lots of music, lots of food, maybe a thousand peo-ple, just an all-around good memorial service," said Doerner. "We didn't have any proof of where he was. Pops took it pretty bad, the whole family was hurt. Everyone was hurt. No one could believe this. It happened too fast."

There is much to be learned, the historians say, from a Hawaiian name. The spelling was inconsequential in ancient times, but by its sound you could tell who a man was, what he was, what district he came from. And there is considerable evidence that "Aikau" is directly related to the ocean. There is *aku*, a type of fish, and *aka*, meaning fish in their transparent, spiritual form. The word *akai* means, simply, "by the sea."

Just recently, I came across an article in the November 1976 *Surfer* by Kimo Hollinger, a big-wave rider and friend of the family. He had enjoyed the privilege of attending one of the Aikaus' fabled *luaus* in the hills above Honolulu. They lived—and still do—on the grounds of a Chinese graveyard, of which they are the caretakers.

"The Aikaus long ago decided what part of western civilization they wanted, and the rest they disregarded," he wrote. "What they kept is blended in with their Maui beginnings to produce a vintage that can only be called 'Hawaiian Folk.'" Hollinger mentioned the likes of Buffalo Keaulana, Conrad Cunha, Larry Bertleman, Peter Cole and Ricky Grigg at the luau. As Grigg said recently, "The spirit of old Hawaii was in that home, and surely still is. Pops maintained that feeling by making people feel good and feel love for each other."

Pops, wrote Hollinger, "stands about five feet, nine inches. He is dark, but so are a lot of other Hawaiians. He walks with a limp, the result of an accident when he stevedored on the Honolulu docks. Nothing about his physical appearance suggests his character except his eyes. When you see them, you know you're in for it. They dance. His voice, on a scale of ten, registers fifteen. He never sits still. If there is no action, he creates it. He usually sports a surfing T-shirt, a pair of jeans and construction shoes, an outfit for action. Wherever he goes, he is usually accompanied by his entourage. The cast changes, but always remains colorful. A couple of this cast invariably belong to the 'heavy' category. This is to ensure that whatever Pop

decrees is understood by all. The others might be from anywhere or anything, but they all have this in common. They are
all caught up in Pop's charisma."

Of Mrs. Aikau, Henrietta, he wrote, "To see her is to see
the soul of the Hawaiian people, a race tempered by the soft
trade winds and the warm Pacific Ocean."

The Aikau family had already known tragedy. Another
son, Gerry, a Viet Nam veteran and a surfer of lesser ability
than Eddie or Clyde, was killed in an auto accident in the early
'70s. "They said Gerry had been Mom's favorite," said
Hollinger. "At that time, the whole family, the other four sons
and the daughter, all moved back in with Mom and Pop."

Doerner has grown especially close to the Aikau family.
He's a lifeguard and big-wave rider—two pretty strong credentials—but the association runs deeper than that. I've been
aware of Darrick since he was a little kid in Malibu, and he's
different. He has an understanding of the ocean that few will
ever grasp, and there's a quiet strength about him that
Hawaiian surfers, in particular, appreciate. Back in the mid-
'70s, he was welcomed into the *Hui O He'e Nalu* ("Group of
men of the sea"), the intensely local surf club that became
known as the Black Shorts. When a criminal element threatened to undermine the *Hui* (several of its members were
jailed, on various charges), Darrick helped restore it as a more
respectable institution, in charge of North Shore water patrol.

Darrick would probably be lost in the conventional world,
with its maze of bankers, accountants and insurance salesmen,
and he couldn't be happier about that. His life is pure surf,
pure style and good times—a Hawaiian lifestyle to the core. As
we talked at the base of the Waimea lifeguard tower in
February '90, he spoke of visiting the Aikau home, being
advised that Eddie's old room has been preserved intact. Not
one thing has been touched. Then he told a story that gave *me*
the chills.

Darrick Doerner

Pops Aikau passed away in late October, 1989. He had withstood the pain of untold grief—the death of one son, then another, and the passing of his beloved wife—and finally, his own life gave out. Darrick had seen Pops just a few days before the end, and he remembers the great man saying, "Big surf coming. Two weeks from now."

On November 2, right on cue, it happened.

Pops was to be buried in Honolulu that day, and Doerner was prepared. He had a specially-made set of flowers, from the rich *maile lei* vine, to present as an offering from the *Hui O He'e Nalu*. But around 2 that morning, he was awakened by the sound of pounding surf outside his house at Backyards. As he stepped out for a first-hand look, he saw nothing but whitewater, everywhere—and he knew. It would be Waimea at dawn.

Now, you won't find too many people surfing 30-foot Waimea Bay before the sun comes out. The place is just too formidable; it requires thought and study. Nobody in his right mind would charge out there on "dawn patrol," like a bunch of guys at the Malibu pier. But Darrick Doerner knows the Bay as few have ever known it. He's the first one out, every time it gets big. And once he's up, in the middle of the night, he can't get back to sleep.

"I was amping," he recalled. "Around 4 a.m., I got in my car and drove down there. I'd called Mark Foo the night before, because I knew it was coming up, and I told him to be

143

ready. I dropped down to his place around 5:30 and honked my horn, made all kinds of noise. 'Foo-Dog!' But, nothing. No lights. So I drove back and parked up on the hill."

With about a dozen *leis* around his neck, Doerner watched a 30-foot closeout set greet the morning's first light. He checked his watch. Just ten minutes later, *another* closeout set arrived, breaking completely across the bay. Whitewater was pushing up past the beach, into the river, onto the grass, and as Eddie always said, you don't surf Waimea under those conditions. But Darrick already had his board. He had a brand-new mission that day. He was walking toward the corner, getting ready to go out.

"I was blind," he says. "Either I pulled it off, or... I got slaughtered."

With absolutely no evidence that the place was rideable, Doerner waited some 20 minutes for a lull and hit the water, the flowers still draped around him. "I didn't fool around, I headed straight out the middle," he said. "I remember the incredible quiet, paddling out. I knew this is what I'd spent the whole summer for, all the training, all the paddling and running on the beach—for *this* day."

Up on the hillside, he spotted his friend Michael Ho, making the kind of gesture that said, "No way." A few other onlookers had arrived. It was around 6:40 now, and Doerner was heading toward the lineup, alone. "My heart was just pounding, and the flowers were startin' to slow me down," he said. "All of a sudden I hear five or six horns goin' off. They could see it coming on the horizon. I paddled over a *solid* 30-foot wave, then two more, just scratching to get over that ledge. And then it was quiet again."

Breathing a little easier, he worked his way over to the takeoff spot. He saw a gigantic turtle, "big as my car." He saw the moon in one direction, the rising sun in another. He cast aside the flowers, suddenly looking gorgeous in the fresh new light. The ritual, spontaneous and spectacularly appropriate, was finished.

144

"I rode a dozen *big* waves with nobody out," he said. "No one *around*. It was the peak of my life, without a doubt. I wound up surfing the whole day—30 waves, 40, maybe even 50, at 20-25 feet. I lost count. About a week later, Clyde came down and I told him the story: about Pop predicting the swell, about the flowers, everything…he had to sit down. He started crying. It was *heavy*. Chicken skin just popping out of his body. I had it, too. I still do."

This is why so many people are talking about 33-year-old Darrick Doerner at Waimea Bay. Because of that day, November 2, and many others. Ask any of the contemporary riders about the most impressive surfing they've seen at Waimea over the last 10 years, and they're bound to mention Doerner. He might have the deepest, most committed relationship with the place since Eddie himself.

I didn't know Darrick that well in the Malibu days. I've got about 10 years on him, so he was always in a different crowd. But I distinctly remember him surfing Zero, a North Malibu spot now overrun with flakes, kooks and pretenders. It was a secret, almost sacred spot back then, a place where we could really let it out, in the pleasure of our own company. Occasionally, a visitor would be welcome. There was one day in the early '60s when Donald Takayama, one of the sport's most legendary names, stopped by and staged a hot-dog performance that re-shaped everyone's thinking. But the place had a locals-only, neighborhood feel, and I can still see Darrick, maybe 11 or 12 years old, just *streaking* across those 8-foot faces (we're talking California size now) in the heat of a summer south swell. He was a brash kid, a tad on the rowdy side, and he could really surf.

"It was all he wanted to do," recalls his father, Vic, who lives on the Big Island. "That was his love. Most guys were out trying to seduce girls in the neighborhood. Darrick was looking for waves."

I caught Darrick in one of the more stable periods of his youth, a five-year span when his family lived just a few houses

145

down from mine. But the separation of his parents found him traveling around the country, around the *world*, to fit the circumstances of the moment. He was born in Fresno, a mid-valley California city known mostly for its Holiday-Inn variety of sophistication. But before he was 15, he had lived in Texas, Maine, North Carolina, even France for two years. [His mother is French, thus the unusual spelling of his first name. "Dah-REEK," he says with a smile.] The mention of "school" brings nothing but bleak memories for him: "Bad neighborhoods, bad kids, scrapes, Ds and Fs."

The basic law in Darrick's family was that he wouldn't be able to make his own decisions until he turned 16. Finally, he did, and he went to Hawaii. Case closed. He's been there ever since.

The real catalyst in his surfing development was Vic, a lifeguard himself in his prime. Vic started surfing the Ventura-Santa Barbara area around 1940-41, joining some of the sport's earlier pioneers. "Yeah, I remember a spot we used to surf called Three Mile," he says. "They call it Rincon now." Before long, such Santa Monica surfers as Peter Cole, Buzzy Trent and Ricky Grigg would be making excursions to Malibu, riding the glorious point waves in relative solitude. And they would all congregate at the renowned Ventura Overhead when the waves got big.

"I've always felt that when a man of any age goes out there and rides a wave, it builds his personal confidence," Vic says. "For anything in life. Nothing else can raise your self-esteem that high. Maybe a college professor can give you confidence, but not as much as surfing, where it's just between you and nature. Even if you make a mistake and the wave busts you, it doesn't matter! That's part of the education, too."

So, while other kids would be catching hell for their surfing, Darrick had it made. Vic would actually watch him from the deck of their house, shooting film, ringing a bell to warn Darrick of an oncoming set. Too cool.

"I left Malibu and moved over here [Kona] about 23 years

ago," says Vic, now 64, still seriously active as a deep-sea diver and cyclist. "I remember Darrick was living with his mother in North Carolina when he turned 16, and he came over here for just a short visit. He went back home for maybe five, six weeks. Then he came right back, saying he wanted to finish high school here. I knew that was BS. He just wanted to surf. I've seen other young men do the same thing. They'll beg, borrow or steal to live in Hawaii, and that's what Darrick did."

He spent about a year and a half on the Big Island, befriending David Kahanamoku, a descendant of the great Duke, and blending well into the local scene. "I guess I grew real close to the people," he says. "Although I'm from somewhere else, I know the right way to approach people wherever I am. I know to be calm, not boisterous, and you get along the best that way.

"I loved the Big-Island waves when they came up, but it didn't happen often enough. Maui, Molokai, Lanai, they all get in the way [of swells]. By the time they hit the Big Island, they're *pau*. So David and I came to the North Shore in the fall of '75, right at Log Cabins, and every time Waimea broke, we were *on* it. We were just little kids then, sitting right next to Eddie Aikau. I dug it. The Hawaiians charged, and I fit right in with 'em. I charged."

Because of that, Doerner got plenty of help. "Jim Soutar showed me around Sunset. He's been surfing it 25, 30 years, and he knows it inside and out. But Tiger Espere was the one who taught me no fear. He would go on *anything*. And whenever I was in the lineup, he'd be screaming, 'Go, brudda! Go, brudda!' That's how it used to be. And when somebody tells you that, you're gonna go. Otherwise you sit there all summer goin', 'I shoulda gone on that wave.' So I went."

I had no idea Darrick was even in Hawaii, much less charging it, until I saw him on the beach at Log Cabins one afternoon in '76. Then it all hit home. The entire right side of his face was covered in bandages; he looked like he'd been pulled out of a terrible car wreck. Turned out he'd been surf-ing Log Cabins, on a particularly dangerous day, when he was pulverized by another board. "It was some military guy," he said. "I was punching under an 8-foot, top-to-bottom wave when the guy got pitched. I saw his board coming, and it was hairline, so I jumped off my board and dove underneath. But the reef was there; nowhere to go. His board just nailed me."

Darrick remained conscious for a moment, just long enough to feel his cheekbone and find nothing but mush. "My hand went in, like, two inches," he says. "The next thing I knew, I was waking up in a helicopter. I had a broken jaw, bro-ken cheekbone, I needed 123 stitches in all. I really feel I'm lucky to be alive. Did you ever hear of Hawaiian *mana*? A friend of mine, Jerry Santos, was up partying in the yard, and he saw me crawling up the beach. He ran down there, took his shirt off and wrapped it around my head, called the ambu-lance for me. I was real lucky he was around. I was out of the water for 8-9 months after that."

He became a North Shore lifeguard that spring, right after getting his jaw unwired. "In those days, it was first aid, CPR, senior lifesaving, and here you go, buddy. Oh, you don't have 'em? Well, get 'em. You're gonna work right now. Today, you need a driver's license, social security number, no warrant out for your arrest [laughter], pass a strenuous physical, and plenty guys in line."

Before moving into the prime zones of Sunset and Waimea, which he occupies today, Doerner worked with Butch Van Artsdalen at Haleiwa. Everyone knew about Butch's drink-ing. They knew he was wasting away. But Butch rode Pipeline in the days when all but about eight people in the world were terrified of the place. He rode it calmly, artistically, even com-ically — spinning around to look back in the tube one moment, riding on his butt the next. One story has him taking off on fifteen consecutive 12-foot closeouts at Haleiwa, power-turning into the lip of each one, just for the sake of getting outrageously thrashed. People cut Butch a lot of slack.

"One day a friend of Butch's died, and they had a funeral at Haleiwa," Doerner recalled. "That was the last day Butchie was sober. Two weeks later, we buried him. The doctors had told him, 'If you do it again, you're history,' because he didn't have any insides left. It was all rotten. But his friends were over there partyin' under the tree, and Butch just couldn't help himself, and two hours later he was back to lookin' like normal, you know? He had the big puffy cheeks [laughs], you could tell he'd been into it, with that milk carton full of vodka-tonic. That was it. Butchie didn't come to work after that. He died up at Wahiawa. His insides just gave way."

Van Artsdalen's lifestyle wasn't so unusual on the North Shore. While people like Ken Bradshaw and Mike Stewart set the good example, hundreds of others like their beer, their weed, and to some extent their cocaine (although its popularity seems to be fading). Doerner has been through that, and he's reached the point where he actively avoids the drug scene.

"I really respect guys like Bradshaw, you know?" said Doerner. "He's never gotten high, never been drunk, he's never fallen, like a lot of us have. He's almost out of touch, in a way. I'm pretty straight now, but I've gone off. And I've been *known* to go off. I've shown up at places at two in the morning, just [contorting his mouth drunkenly]...But it's something I don't like to do, and I stay away from those particular people. We all know, one line leads to another. And another. Before you know it, you're pounding beers, and you're doing more, and next thing you know it's three in the morning—and you've gotta *work* the next day. Oh, is that a dead-end street.

"Couple years ago, I sucked all kinds of beers. Work eight hours in the hot sun, man, six beers...*gone*. Wake up and do it again the next day. I did that for five or six years, six-pack every day. North Shore, man. North Bore. Now, on the weekends maybe, I'll have a beer. But I stay away from the dust. That's my advice to anyone. Doesn't matter who you are, you can't control it."

Doerner doesn't really need to prove anything about his lifestyle. He proves it with his all-day power surfing in 25-foot waves, with his dawn-patrol approach, with his windsurfing and lifeguarding. "This guy's definitely one of the 10 fittest guys on the North Shore," says longtime surf-contest judge Jack Shipley. And Doerner has saved countless lives, in every conceivable way.

"The heaviest rescues are at Sunset when you realize it's 15 feet, with 20-foot sets, no channel left, and all you can do is go outside, all the way around to Backyards," said Doerner. "That's an hour-and-a-half session. Ross Clarke-Jones [the Australian big-wave surfer] was a good example. He got nailed by a board out there and punctured his lung, broke a few ribs. He was a good three-quarters of a mile out. By the time I got there, he was in shock. Couldn't breathe, couldn't get on my rescue board; he was just puking blood. Mark Foo and Charlie Walker were with him, and they wanted to cut back to the channel, against the current. But it was a west swell—big, giant peaks—and if we were cuttin' across and a big set hit Ross, he'd die.

"I waved off the helicopter and decided to fight the rip out just a little bit farther, like 200 feet, then head over to the channel at Velzyland. That's where my windsurfing comes in; I know exactly where to come in through there. Mark wound up gettin' picked off and swimming in, but Charlie hung right with me, because he knew it was gettin' too big over there. I had Ross on his knees, with his hands behind his neck, because that's how he could breathe the best. We timed it just right between sets. Perfect. Came right in between Backyards and Velzyland. When I hit the beach and looked around, Sunset was 20 feet. Just history."

For several years, Doerner has tucked a swim fin inside the back of his vest, just as a safeguard when Sunset and Waimea get out of control. He's bailed out a lot of struggling surfers by offering them that fin, and he's bailed himself out, too. "Stick that thing on, and you're gone. *Right* into the whitewater. *Right* up to the beach. *So* fast. Without a fin, you've got a lot of kickin' to do, man. It gets insane out there."

It seems that wherever water men are performing at the highest level around the North Shore, there's Doerner. He entered the Fourth of July paddling contest from Sunset to Waimea one year, just for the fun of it, and wound up winning. He windsurfs the Sunset-Backyards area at 15 feet—think about *that* for a minute—with his buddies Richard Schmidt, Paul Dunn, Charlie Smith and Clyde Aikau, and there are huge callouses on his hands from the strain of that endeavor. His surfing, of course, speaks for itself.

"Darrick has all the attributes," says Ricky Grigg. "He's wiry, built like a cheetah—light, but extremely strong. His muscles are like steel wires. He's perfectly suited for big-wave riding, because you don't want to be too big. You need paddling ability, explosive strength, high agility, and of course, you have to be fearless. Maybe crazy. Darrick probably qualifies in all of those categories."

Derek Hynd, the fine Australian journalist, caused a stir on the North Shore one winter with his interpretation of big-wave riders' motivation. Bradshaw, he said, did it for the machismo; Foo for the glory. Both men took great exception to that. But Hynd said Doerner did it for "the cool," and Darrick didn't mind at all. "It *is* cool," he says. "I've felt that from the first day I watched Eddie Aikau at the Bay. Even if he had white skin, you could tell he was Hawaiian, because he had ultimate Hawaiian style. Take off and drop in, lay out this *big* bottom turn, appear out of mountains of whitewater, pop out, throw his hair back...that's Eddie. He surfed bow-legged. Bully style. That's Hawaiian all the way. And Eddie had the meanest local style. Nobody dropped in on him. If they had that in mind, they *asked* him first.

"It's still cool out there, especially when it's just the five of us—myself, Kenny, Brock, Roger Erickson, Mark Foo. And occasionally you'll see Tony Roy, Tommy Nellis, Dennis Pang, Bobby Owens, Keone Downing. They're all into it. Michael Ho and Johnny Boy, too, when they're on it. Sometimes Kenny'll get a little uptight, and I'll throw some shit at him. Like, *big* set's coming, and I'll be, "OK, Kenny, now, now, OK, no, no, back off, back off... GO! [laughter] Kenny's a little bit off in his timing sometimes."

Doerner reserves special respect for Peter Cole, the age-less one in the white shirt, knee-paddling into that *certain* wave he's been waiting for. "Now, that's what I want to be," said Darrick. "I'm gonna be out there knee-paddling, and the young kids better respect me. I hope I'm not half-blind, like he is [a degenerative condition left Cole with the use of only one eye]. He gets scared, the way I get scared. He doesn't like people, because people make him wipe out. So when you see Peter, you get everybody out of his way, he'll go, and he'll have a beautiful wave. He's so happy, and he'll thank everybody on his way back out.

"But man, the pros just burn that guy. They eat him up. They snake him [voice growing bitter], pull up underneath him, and they know he's gonna pull out. That's just crude. I see that and I back the guys off. Hey, where's your respect, you know? Get the *fuck* out of the way. Give this guy a wave. But no, you've gotta say something first. You gotta give a ticket. Like Soutar, he's out there givin' tickets all day long. Like [loud whistle], 'Come here! You know what you just did?'"

Doerner doesn't mind foreign surfers on the North Shore, as long as they show a little tact. There's an art to get-ting a feel for Sunset, sort of soaking up the knowledge, with-out ruining the day for others. Darrick doesn't feel the Japanese have quite figured that out. "I get tired of these guys sitting inside, and then *just* as you catch it, they turn around and snake you. And I like those guys, you know? But I've had it up to here. I had this incident where I dropped in, went to the bottom, and this Japanese guy drops in front of me. OK, give me an inch, then. Just an inch. No. Not even an inch. He wait-ed for the last possible second, and then laid it out. And see, I *dream* about Sunset. To get cut off by a foreigner, no.

"I didn't swim in. I swam after him. And I got him. Hit him with my hand open, turned his board over…is there a fin there? Great, man [ripping sound]. Fins are gone! There's my peace. Right to 'em. *You. My* board.

"I go that far. Kenny, hell, they don't go near him. They call him Nek Wahsdarb. That's his name backwards. So we keep an eye on those guys, big-time. They surf like we play chess. Every little move we don't do, they're gonna come *right* up in there."

What people don't realize, he says, is that's there's no room for amateurs at a place like Sunset. The consequence is just too great. "That's the worst punishment," he says. "Waimea's a heavy deal, but Sunset, it don't let you go. It just sucks you back into the whitewater, throws you through Boneyards, you hit the bottom, you jump back up, it throws you right back down. And you know there's five or six waves comin'. Sunset just scares the shit out of me…You're a little bit inside, you paddle hard for a wave, *just* miss it, and then there's a 15-foot set feathering on the outside, and you ain't gonna get there. Scariest thing in the *world*."

You'll see Doerner wearing a leash occasionally, but he didn't even acknowledge them until the late '80s. When 33 surfers paddled out into all-time Waimea Bay for the 1990 Eddie Aikau contest, Doerner was the only one not wearing a cord. He was just loving it, too.

"Cords slow you down, wherever you are," he says. "I have a box full of 'em, but most of the time I like not having one. Used to be, your ability defined the lineup. If you weren't ready to swim in, you weren't out there. Simple as that. Remember those days, when you looked out for the other guy's board? Guys swimming in and running up the beach? Just the natural order of things. Allows the other guys to catch a few waves. Now, you've got a wave-hog problem. You got guys bein' all piggy-wiggy out there.

"I think cords are dangerous, too. We had a 25-foot day at Waimea about three years ago, and I saw Foo go for the first wave of this set...and miss it. He turned around and saw our eyes, and we saw his. And all we saw was him get *sucked* [makes a noise of anguish]. He said he didn't pop up until he was all the way inside. Went through the water like an egg-beater, with his board and his cord. We didn't see him for about 30 minutes. He sat on the beach for a while, paddled back out, and we *knew*, man. The cord just dragged him into insanity.

"People say, 'Oh, but cords help you out if you make a mistake.' No. That's wrong. To me, guys who wear leashes aren't 100 percent mentally. Guys like me and Roger, Peter Cole and Billy Sickler and David Kahanamoku, we don't go out there figurin' we're gonna make mistakes. I'm *not* gonna make one. I'm gonna ride four hours without losing this board."

Four hours at 25-foot Waimea without a mistake. All *day* at Waimea without a mistake. You begin to understand why this guy is just a little bit ahead of the rest. I was on the North Shore on January 31, 1988, but like just about everyone else, I was watching the Super Bowl. That turned out to be the day Darrick caught the biggest wave of his life—maybe the biggest by anyone in all of the 1980s.

"I was having a barbecue at my chick's house at Ke Iki that day," he recalls. "Everyone was drinkin' and partyin', and I was just watching it get bigger. It was maybe three feet in the morning. Now it's coming up, big-time, and around 1 o'clock it's 15 feet, but the game's on. Next thing you know I'm watchin' Chief's Ledge, outside Jose Angel's old place. It was goin' off, 20 feet. A half-hour later it was 25 feet. Just solid whitewater from Ke Iki all the way to V-Land. All gone. And I almost got a speeding ticket goin' home to get my stick. Fuck Super Bowl Sunday, fuck the barbecue, fuck everything. I'm goin' surfing."

Three feet in the morning. By 3 p.m., Doerner, Bradshaw and Little were paddling over 30-foot sets. That's nowhere but Hawaii.

"It took us an hour to just get out there, and it was *closing*," he said. "We didn't even come close to paddling for 'em. We just dodged waves for an hour and a half, and we were gettin' tired of it."

Mike Latronic was on the scene, a man who rides Sunset as big as it gets, but he wasn't ready for this. "I was on the beach with a brand-new, 9-foot Rawson, and I wasn't sure of my equipment," he said. "I was just watching it, and I think that's the most scared I've ever been. Just a full-gut fear. Those guys were *animals*, being out there. I tried getting out and just got shut down immediately. The whole bay closed out. I got my courage up, got nailed, and just came in."

Finally, a set arrived with just a slightly different look. Darrick was on it. "Kenny was around there somewhere," he said. "He said he could have had it, but he realized I'd picked it up outside. And when I went over the edge, they kissed me off. They all did. That's it for Darrick. But I pulled it off. The drop was just a *blur* to me. It still is. I remember at some point on that wave I heard about 50 car horns. People were all over the place, yellin' 'Go for it!' and when I turned around and went, they went *off*. The *mana* was *heavy*.

"You get a little airborne on the drop when it's that size," he said. "You can count on that. But my windsurfing taught me how to take off and land, and land straight. And I made the drop. I made the *turn*. I made the whole wave on a 9-6 Brewer, and it was a good, pumpin' 30-foot wave."

That was the critical difference, his actually surfing the wave. Not taking off and cascading into oblivion, but riding it successfully. Later, Peter Cole would say, "He rode it very, very well, and he was airborne for half the drop. It reminded me of Pat Curren and Buzzy Trent, that wave. The most impressive I've seen in the past 10 years."

Down on the beach, up on the cliff, people were stunned by the sight of this accomplishment. "It was just beautiful and perfect," said Tom Nellis, who had gotten the wave of *his* life that day. "And it couldn't have been surfed any better. There is no more expertise. I've seen a lot of big waves go by that I could have ridden, believe me. Darrick's was a hoss. I mean, it was a big dude. That guy's got balls, man. He's something. He's different."

It wasn't exactly a fairy-tale ending, because after Doerner made his bottom turn, got around the corner and began riding toward the middle of the Bay, he got annihilated. "I went over this giant Aikau bounce [laughter], managed to straighten out, and then I ate it," he said. "Just too much whitewater."

Darrick didn't have his emergency fin that day. In fact, a couple of years had gone by since he'd worn it. But a truly amazing thing happened when he came to the surface. "I popped up, and there was this fin," he said. "Just right in front of me, floating there. It was an Extra Small, and I'm a Large, but it went *on*, man. And you would have done it, too. I just switched it from foot to foot."

I ventured a comment: "Maybe Eddie left it for you."

"Yeah. It was an omen. Really a strange thing. I've got that fin nailed inside our [lifeguard] locker room."

When Doerner got to the beach, he said, "There were people everywhere. It was like a supermarket. Everyone came down drunk from the Super Bowl. I was weaving and grinding through hundreds of people, and they're goin', 'Oh, wow, that was *heavy*, brah.'"

And it was just about the most incredible moment of his life…until that November 2, the day of Pops Aikau's funeral. And Doerner's ritual that morning was only half the story. People still talk about Doerner's performance that day, and they don't even *know* about the flowers, the closeout sets and his pre-sunrise surfing. That's because he surfed the place all day long—as he said, 30 or 40 or *50* rides. He came in just once, when he saw his good friend Kahanamoku crawling up the beach, both hands in the sand, but with one foot trailing in the air. A collision with another board had broken David's leg in two places, and Doerner helped get him to the hospital. Not only that, he gave a huge assist to Little, who was out of breath and in big trouble, by handing him the trusty swim fin. "I'm not sure Brock would have gotten in without it," said

Doerner. "It would have taken him another three tries around the Bay."

What made Doerner's session so remarkable was that just about everyone else bailed out to Makaha that day. "Waimea was really big, and the reports had it getting bigger," said Foo. "It started closing out. I went out there and got cleaned, man. If I'd been a little closer to the impact of this one wave, I would have died. Just that simple. I have never been more worried. It was so big, even Darrick was talking about Makaha."

Foo wound up hitting the West side with Dennis Pang. "I'd always wanted to surf Makaha," he said. "I'd never been out there when it was big, so I figured this was my chance. It was pretty amazing, just 15 feet and *perfect*. But I couldn't stand it, I couldn't concentrate. It wasn't Waimea. That's all I could think about, getting back to Waimea. I wound up hitch-hiking back."

And there he found Doerner, just riding and riding and riding. "Darrick told me he rode some of the best waves of his life that day," said Foo. "And that means something, because that guy has taken off on waves that most mortals could not even imagine. By the end of the day, he'd commanded so much respect that Dick Brewer gave him three new guns. He was like a super-human out there."

In his excellent work, "The Legend of Eddie Aikau," Nick Carroll quotes Clyde Aikau about a November day in 1967, when Eddie came into his own at the Bay. The waves were a consistent 30 feet, he said, some of them bigger. "Everyone was out that day," said Clyde. "George Downing, Felipe Pomar, Greg Noll, you know. And Eddie was just a normal Hawaiian guy who nobody knew, who just paddled out there and totally dominated the whole day. It's incredible how one day can change your entire life."

"That's exactly it," Doerner says now. "That one day changed my life. It was the culmination of everything I've done in surfing. That's *me* out there, that's what I'm about. I've never felt closer to myself than when it's 25, 30 feet. It's meditation to me. I get back on land, I stub my toe, I trip. Whereas out there, it's just...perfect. All the elements come together, and there is no fear."

The Eddie

On the morning of January 21, 1990, I saw Mike Stewart leaving the water at Waimea Bay. Word was beginning to spread that after four years, the Eddie Aikau contest would finally be going off, but Stewart had his doubts. "It's too small," he said as he walked up the Kam Highway. "They shouldn't hold it."

A lot of the competitors were feeling the same way. A rare, southeast wind was gracing the North Shore, the type that blows straight offshore, but few of the sets were pushing 20 feet. What could they be thinking?

By the end of the day, it became evident why George Downing was left in charge of this contest. Trusting his buoy readings and the advice of forecasters, he alerted everyone for an 11 a.m. start—and the waves arrived on cue. The surf was a solid 18 to 25 feet for most of the day, with a couple of sets pushing 30, and the result might have been the best contest ever held at Waimea Bay. It was an absolutely brilliant call.

"There have only been six Waimea contests in the 25 years I've been judging," said Jack Shipley. "The 1974 and '75 Smirnoff contests stand out, and the '86 Billabong. But this was in the top three. In fact, I'd put it right behind the '74 contest, because it was consistently bigger that year. But this day was so *clean*. It rarely gets that clean. And I mean, rarely."

Oceanographer Ricky Grigg had seen the swell coming, noting on his charts that a huge storm off Japan was colliding with a typhoon off Guam. He figured the biggest sets would arrive around 2 p.m., and that's exactly what happened. "Some of the sets were just mind-boggling," he said a few days later. "The direction was much more west than we usually get. It made the waves really thick and ledgy, and when you add those offshore winds, it made it very difficult to drop in. Really dramatic stuff."

Mark Foo described the day as "all-time epic." Richard Schmidt put it in his "top three" over the last 10 years. Darrick Doerner said it reminded him of a day when he surfed 15-18-foot Laniakea with Wayne Lynch in howling offshores, "tubes so big you could build a house in both directions," and a level of excitement so great, he was hoarse from yelling. Personally, I felt a sense of privilege to be on the beach. I'd blown off the Super Bowl (January 28) months in advance, because the two-week delay always struck me as one of the dumbest, most pretentious stunts ever pulled in professional sports. I could either sit around for 14 days, being an idiot, waiting for yet another stale Super Bowl, or get on with my North Shore vacation. And there I was, watching one of the best surfing contests ever staged. I felt like my very existence had been validated.

Befitting the Aikau tradition, the contest had a special atmosphere. Instead of the usual junk-rock music, inevitably played too loud, the sound of a solitary drumbeat came through the loudspeaker, with a foreboding, heavily Polynesian kind of feel. The sense of anticipation was every-where — and the field of 33 entrants was unfolding into a Hawaiian dream.

There had been one change from the original list. Aaron Napoleon was pushed into the alternates' sector to make room for Eddie Rothman, former leader of the Black Shorts, as an "Aikau family selection." There was little quarrel with that, at least publicly. It had been Rothman's idea to have a contest in Aikau's name. "He's not really a big-wave surfer, and he tried to give his spot away," Doerner said. "I told him, hey, it's an honor. Go for it. You deserve to be in there."

Titus Kinimaka definitely deserved to be there. He'd been

surfing brilliantly all winter, and people were describing him as a worthy addition to the hard-core Waimea crew. But on Christmas Day, the Kauai standout broke his leg at Waimea, and nearly drowned in the aftermath. Witnesses said the lip of an 18-foot wave landed directly on Kinimaka's right thigh as he pulled up from his bottom turn. Ken Bradshaw said he couldn't believe a wave could do that much damage; the femur bone was shattered, coming right out of the hip socket. "I've got to believe Titus' board was involved somehow," he said. But when Bradshaw, Doerner and a few others pulled a badly shaken Kinimaka out of the water, they knew he'd be through for the winter. "His leg was so swollen, it was the size of your waist," said Doerner.

As much as Quiksilver wanted a strong representation from the pro tour, it was almost non-existent. Tom Carroll, Gary Elkerton, Martin Potter and Wes Laine had all gone home—and they could hardly be blamed, since the ASP takes its break in January and February. Shaun Tomson, who had just finished his last full season on the tour, was missing. So were three other former world champs: Tom Curren, Mark Richards and Rabbit Bartholomew. Simply not around. After watching three winters pass with no Eddie contest, they were probably wondering if it would *ever* be held.

Marvin Foster was the final no-show. He was on the island, but a mixup in communications left him too late to surf his first heat. So there were 10 spots open, in all, and that opened the way for some very deserving Hawaiian alternates: Reno Abellira, Owl Chapman, Johnny Boy Gomes, Kerry Terukina (described by Mark Foo as the current best at Haleiwa), Mel Kini, Louis Ferreira, Lance Hookano, Napoleon and Ronnie Burns, whose death in a trail-bike accident would leave the surfing community in shock just six months later. Barton Lynch, the Australian world champion of '88, was still in Hawaii and filled the final position.

It would have been interesting to see the likes of Carroll, Curren and Elkerton at Waimea, but on the real side, they weren't missed. This turned into a pure Hawaiian contest, to the delight of just about everyone on the beach. Incredibly, at a spot that was pioneered by West Coast surfers, there was only one Californian—Schmidt, who generally spends the entire winter on the North Shore. Only three Australians were on hand: Lynch, Cheyne Horan and Ross Clarke-Jones, all of whom surfed commendably. And there was a single Japanese surfer, Takao Kuga, who turned a lot of heads with some forthright surfing and finished in a tie for 14th.

"Kuga was charging it," said Randy Rarick. "I was really surprised, because generally, the Japanese are intimidated in big waves. They're so far down in the pecking order, it's very difficult for them to get established. But this guy just said, 'Hey, I've got nothing to lose,' and went for it. Maybe not the biggest waves, but he was going for it. That was the best performance I've seen by the Japanese over here."

Downing's format was unusual and refreshing: three heats of 11 men each, surfing for an hour, with a four-wave limit. No eliminations. Then three more heats, with different combinations of 11. Score each man's four best rides for the day, then add it all up. "I thought 11 guys was way too many," Bradshaw said later. "It's absurd, having that many capable guys in the lineup at one time. But you can't complain about surfing for two hours, at two different times of the day, and realistically, you couldn't cut down the field. There would be too many complaints. I thought the format was very fair. They can't improve on it."

They could, however, make some other changes. The distribution of prize money was laughable: $55,000 to the winner, $10,000 for second place, $5000 for third, then a lousy $350 for everybody else. Here you've got the world's greatest big-wave riders putting their lives on the line, in a contest they've been anticipating for years, and only three of them get rewarded? The hefty first prize is great—long overdue for the sport. But surfing two hours at serious Waimea Bay is worth at least $2000 for everybody, right down to 33rd place. "I mean, if you didn't have a shot at the top three, you could just hang it up," said Bradshaw. "There was no more incentive."

Waimea is also a very difficult spot for judging. Shipley had his regular crew (with Barry Kanaiaupuni a welcome addition) on the scaffolding near the lifeguard tower, and they did an excellent job under the circumstances. But you can only see so much from the beach. With a huge set in progress, you're lucky to catch the takeoffs on the outside waves. "My best wave was completely missed," claimed Mark Foo. "I saw photos and videos of it later, one of the heaviest drops I've ever had out there. I scored like a 30 on it, and Hans Hedemann, who was in front of me, scored an 80.

"I'm totally disappointed," said Foo. "I don't think it was deliberate, they just missed it. What can you do when there's 20-foot sets, three waves in front, the judges 200 yards away, not high enough off the ground, and all in one place? You need guys on the point, to really see who's riding what, and you need guys up on the cliff."

Not only that, it's impossible to hand out 11 distinct colors in a heat. You can't really say, "Burnt Sienna, up and riding." So there'd be one surfer in blue, another in blue and black, and was that pink or red out there? The result was a constant flow of misinformation from the public-address system, and the realization that some wondrous surfing was *not* being judged. "They were just guessing," said Rarick.

But as they say around the North Shore, "Minors." No worries. It was the spirit of Eddie Aikau and the surfing that really mattered, and after six hours of truly challenging waves, the performance level was nothing short of historic. Here's how it went:

Heat One: Appropriately, Reno Abellira got the first wave. Back in '74, he had won that epic Smirnoff contest in 25-foot, Thanksgiving-day conditions. He got buried this time. The first three riders all got snuffed in titanic wipeouts.

This heat belonged to Doerner and 43-year-old Roger Erickson, who used their years of experience to great advantage. Darrick caught four 20-plus waves and rode them all expertly, piling up a 261-point total that left everyone in the dust. And when he lost his board (the only surfer in the contest without a leash), Erickson went out of his way to deliver it, trailing it behind him with one foot. A real class move. Erickson also did some outrageous shorebreak riding, staying in one wave as it turned all white and hideous, and finally taking a savage drop into about three feet of water. The judges didn't see much use in that maneuver, but the crowd went nuts. "Yeah, well, it wasn't much," Erickson said on the beach. "Just thrills."

The thrills were just beginning. Terukina got launched off the lip of a legitimate 20-footer and did a top-to-bottom freefall, landing with the crisp expertise of an Acapulco cliff diver. Ferreira took a wipeout so horrendous he barely survived the impact of the next two waves, and as Doerner said, "He was done. His arms were as close to noodles as you can get. I had to go over a set wave with him, so he could get his air."

When the heat was over, I overheard Erickson advising Clyde Aikau as to the lineup and swell direction. I'd never seen much of Clyde, but as so many other surfers told me, he is quite nondescript. He doesn't have the gladiator's body or the matinee-idol's face, and he spoke to Erickson with a stammer. He just looked like another guy on the beach. As always, Clyde would prove otherwise when it came time to get serious.

"It's *so* good out there," Erickson told him.

Heat Two: Heavy heat. Picture yourself as Barton Lynch, sort of new at this game, trying to make a name for yourself against Michael Ho, Owl Chapman, Brock Little, Johnny Boy Gomes, Richard Schmidt, Ken Bradshaw, Brian Keaulana and Dane Kealoha. "I was honored just be out there with all those lunatics," Lynch would say later, with a smile. "There were some crazy blokes out there. *Real* crazy."

They needed all of that craziness to handle what was coming. A massive set approached, three waves strong. "That's up there," said a smiling Grigg as the crowd hooted an unridden monster that even Downing said was pushing 30 feet. "Guys were freakin' out," Bradshaw said later. "I was really upset for not riding one of those, and I know Brock was, too. I don't know if I missed the lineup a little, or I was just too cautious, but I blew that set. Nobody rode any of 'em."

About 20 minutes later, they all got another chance. This time, Little stepped forward. It looked like Napoleon might push over the ledge, and then Bradshaw, but it was Little who went for it. He executed a perfect takeoff, got about two-thirds of the way down…and then simply got hammered, disappearing under an avalanche of Waimea brutality.

"He stepped into the unridden realm," Foo said. "That was a 30-footer. Only a few other guys have ever been in that situation. Brock was in early, he stayed low, he did everything right. It just gets to a stage where it can't be ridden. There's too much water. You're too insignificant. There's just no way you can get to the bottom by the time the lip comes over."

"That was just amazing, what Brock did," said Foo. "Most guys run from those waves, but Brock is fearless. He's always been fearless."

And he's only 22 years old. The way Brock Little rips small waves, 10-foot waves, 18-foot waves, and then steps in the Waimea arena with such remarkable tranquility, there's a pretty good chance he'll be the best all-around surfer in Hawaii within a few years. He might be there now.

"Brock's young and just on fire," Doerner said a full year before the contest. "He's having fun. He could catch 4-5 waves, as big as he's ever ridden, and win the whole thing easily."

The heat was a triumph for Gomes, whose 223 points ranked first among some very exclusive company. Kealoha came in at 182, a higher total than Ho, Bradshaw or Chapman, but he wasn't comfortable with what he'd seen. When the time came for Kealoha's second heat, he wasn't around.

"Dane and Michael didn't want any part of that wave Brock took off on," said Foo. "I don't think Dane's ever seen a wave like that. He came in and said, 'It's not worth fifty grand,' and left. He didn't go back out...Dane Kealoha, man. He's a legend."

"It wasn't his cup of tea," said Bradshaw. "The guy's an unbelievable Pipeline surfer, Backdoor surfer. Unbelievable tube rider. But when it gets over 15 feet, that's another story. I thought what Dane did was smart. Nobody should surf anywhere if they aren't comfortable. No kind of pressure should make you feel otherwise."

From Doerner's view, "Dane was in a *bad* place, and he barely made it. When you're scratching over a 25-foot wave sideways, your heart's in your mouth. And you don't even know where your brain is. Dane is a *very* smart person."

As it turned out, Dane drove to Haleiwa for some lunch, got stuck in a massive traffic jam, and returned too late to even watch his next heat. That gave him a built-in excuse for bailing out, but he didn't use it. In an interview months later, Kealoha graciously offered his thoughts about the day, the contest, and his decision to withdraw.

"I was never a Waimea surfer, and I never really wanted to be," he said. "I was born to hot-dog surf, and in my day there wasn't much Waimea surfing going on. Once a year, maybe, it would happen, so it wasn't something I grew up with. I grew up enjoying the waves, not running from them.

"I'm not knocking the event in any way. It's the best thing to happen to Hawaiian surfing in a long time. We held it for a great surfer, one of the greatest in Hawaii since Duke Kahanamoku, and the surfers really gave their lives to that contest. I don't think any athlete in any other sport could have survived something like this."

Kealoha was on the beach with his family when Ferreira took his horrible wipeout. "I grew up with the guy," Dane said. "We've known each other since we were little kids. I saw him come up from that wave, and the second one broke right on him. He barely made it up, and then the third one got him. He was lucky to be alive. If it wasn't for guys like Brian

Keaulana and Darrick, he probably wouldn't have made it. I was sitting there on the beach with my wife and kids, and I just freaked out. To watch one of my best friends almost go...."

When Dane paddled out, he got that funny feeling every surfer experiences when the situation is too extreme. "Even when I surf Backdoor, there are days when I feel I can just conquer the waves, and other days when I have to pull back," he said. "I'm not afraid to say Waimea was pretty hairy that day. When I looked at Michael Ho, Bradshaw and some of the other guys out there, I could see in their eyes that they felt the same way. Guys like Brock really paid the price for the waves they wanted, and they staged a great performance, but even they weren't taking off on the really massive ones that came through."

Dane said he "pretty much went for it" in his heat, but there would be no second round. "I could feel the pressure that was going on out there, and I didn't want to do it again," he said. "By the time I got back from Haleiwa my heat was already gone, but deep down inside, I didn't care. I was happy just being with my family, knowing they wouldn't be worried. Everybody was looking at the prize money, but to me, that wasn't surfing as I know it. It wasn't the kind of surfing my ancestors did in Hawaii. It was more like survival. I just didn't feel it was worth my life."

Heat Three: It seemed inconceivable that anyone could out-surf Doerner. "Look at this," he said, jokingly, looking at the scoreboard. "I'm kickin' everybody's ass." But then came Keone Downing with a staggering 306 points, a textbook Waimea performance that would prove to be critical as the day went on.

Keone is a son of the great George Downing, one of the most respected big-wave riders in surfing history, and he kept his distance from the pre-contest hype. It was seldom you'd even hear his name mentioned. "He's been on it for 15 years, kind of quietly so," said Grigg. "He's always been one of the best, but he's not a guy to talk about it. My sister told me he's

167

been running, training, lifting weights for three years, getting ready for this. That's what he's been all about. Sort of like Rocky Five—this guy's out there training, nobody knows about it, then he comes in and pulls the big knockout. Pretty great."

When I asked Downing about the specifics of his preparation, he said, "Secret. I'm not trying to be some mystery man, there's just no sense people knowing what I do. That's the way it will be, as long as I plan to compete. There will be a time to let them know."

At 36, Downing has a full-time job running the Downing surf shop just outside Waikiki. "He *is* the shop," said Shipley. "And he's one of the best outrigger-canoe riders in all of Hawaii. He and his brother, Kainoa, have been together 15 years in the 8-man canoe paddle from Molokai to Honolulu. That's 37.8 miles, paddling a canoe. Yeah, I'd say he's incredibly fit."

Photographer Warren Bolster, who spends a lot of time on the West side, puts Keone in a class with Brian Keaulana as a water man. "George never pushed his son, he let him do things totally on his own," said Bolster. "One day when Keone was just a kid, George took him out on a huge day at Makaha. Set him up right in the bowl. Said, 'You sit here, I'm paddling outside.' Well, Makaha is known as the worst wipeout there is. A bowl set came in, and Keone nearly drowned. George just came up and said, 'There. Now you can survive anything.'"

Surprisingly, when the Aikau contest arrived, Downing was surfing Waimea for the first time all winter. "I only surf the place when it's 20 feet and clean, which isn't that often," he said. "I have other places I enjoy surfing a lot more—just as big, and less crowded. My brother and I have some places that we know. It's not like I felt I needed to practice there. I've been surfing the Bay since 1973, and it's sort of like riding a bicycle. If you learn it well enough, you never forget."

Downing surfed this heat as if it had been especially designed for him. Even with 10 other men out, he surfed alone. He didn't chase the waves; they found him. All of the true Hawaiian water men, it seems, have this quality. I've come to believe there's an inner level of communication between surfers and the ocean, and there are rewards for those who are most in tune with it. Write it off as some mystical rambling if you'd like, but I've seen too much evidence to the contrary. Loud, obnoxious surfers have their time, and then they crash and burn. People like Downing, Clyde Aikau, Billy Hamilton and Gerry Lopez have the deeper understanding, and they persevere.

"Surfing big waves is not an all-out, aggressive kind of deal, the way you might think," said Doerner. "There's a flow to it. A long time ago, I learned from Henry Declue, a great man from the Makaha side. 'Let it flow,' he said. Don't fight it."

As Downing said a couple of weeks after the contest, "You have to understand that the ocean is a powerful force, and you're just a small element in it. You've got to understand it, be in harmony with it, because it's gonna carry you most of the time. The more you can use it, be with it, have it work in your favor, the easier it becomes."

While Downing, Clyde and Ronnie Burns (in an inspirational backside performance) stood out in the third heat, a video crew showed up embarrassingly late. I also noticed that only one other person on the beach, scribbling in a foreign language, was even taking notes. And the thought struck me: No wonder surfing hasn't caught on as a major sport. You can't *find* it. With a World Series, an Indy 500 or even a weekend downhill-ski race, you've got a pretty good idea where to go, and when. Media people are tripping over themselves. With an event like the Eddie Aikau, or the old Duke contest, you can only wait. The patience can grow thin. And it only heightens your appreciation of these athletes, who live and train for vague, thoroughly random dates on the calendar.

Down on the beach, some jerk, apparently tripping on acid, lurched into the shorebreak wearing a pair of shorts and tennis shoes. He was going to go bodysurfing on a 20-foot day at Waimea Bay, and nobody was going to tell him differently.

Lifeguards Terry Ahue and Mark Dombrowski, becoming increasingly furious, spent several minutes trying to coax the guy out as he splashed and floundered, gesturing rudely in their direction. The scene became a ludicrous sideshow, and when Ahue and Dombrowski finally dragged him onto the sand, they showed professional restraint by not hauling off and belting the guy. He really had it coming.

Up by the tower, Roger Erickson quietly watched the waves, gently holding his infant child.

Heat Four: The historic one. Between 2:20 and 3 p.m., the North Shore audience was treated to some of the greatest Waimea surfing ever. Little, now firmly establishing himself as the day's guttiest rider, kicked it off by pulling into a staggeringly large tube and actually coming out, only to fall off— probably out of shock.

There was bedlam on the beach. Grigg was jumping up and down, shouting. Well-seasoned lifeguards were yelling, 'Hundred points!' It was a *very* heavy deal. "That was red line," said Erickson. "All the way off the scale. You don't do that if you want to surf here a long time. Not judicial at all."

Tube riding at Waimea is hardly new, Booby Jones having pioneered the maneuver way back in the '70s. In the winter of '88-89, during an Aikau expression session, Foo pulled off a sensational ride that brought the notion back into focus. How big was Brock's wave? Probably not in the 20-foot realm. Foo, Bradshaw and many others believe you can't tube-ride Waimea over 18 feet, because by the time you crank a bottom turn on a wave that big, you're a little too late for the barrel. But it was something to see, earning Little a near-perfect score of 98.

"I was thrilled to see it," said Grigg. "For a long time, big-wave riding did not develop like the rest of the sport. It kind of lagged behind. Now we're seeing all that super athleticism and technical innovation making their entry into big-wave riding for the first time. I've been trying to do that my whole life, and I never quite managed. It was nice to see someone finally do what I dreamed about."

Lifeguard Rick Williams, meanwhile, offered some perspective. "I was here for the '74 Smirnoff contest," he said. "It's something that will always stick in my mind. I saw Ricky Grigg take off on a wave that...I was calling it 30 feet. It was the heaviest surf, the heaviest surfers, the ultimate show. But what we're seeing right now...hey, it's *right* up there."

Richard Schmidt was pretty blown away, too. "Tube riding out there is *such* a commitment," he said. "The end shuts down so hard, and the water's just like cement. I've never done what Brock did. I've never even seen it."

Just when the crowd had recovered from the impact of Little's accomplishment, Michael Ho got tubed—and he was in there a *long* time, before it finally collapsed on him. Then Napoleon went for it, backside. Three Waimea tube rides in a 40-minute span. Before the day was over, Lynch and Tony Moniz would be in there, too. While nobody made it out, that was hardly the point.

"You had a lot of positive things working," said Rarick. "One, surfing has progressed. Two, the boards are more maneuverable than ever. Three, you had perfect waves opening up in the offshore winds. And more than anything, you had the contest—the money, the glory, the people on the beach. Guys were just *going* for it."

Doerner closed out this memorable heat with the ultimate cool ride: take the drop, make the wave, ride it in, step right onto the beach without even breaking stride. But Darrick had lost his edge. On the first wave of the heat, he wrenched his right knee trying to leg-save his board inside. Rarick, who was watching from the point, noted that "Darrick wasn't charging it any more; he was holding back." And now the reason was evident. "If you don't have your legs right," said Doerner. "You're in a little bit of trouble at Waimea." He would wear a knee brace for months afterward.

Heat Five: Clyde's heat. It was raining now, and there weren't many waves, but Clyde just willed his way through.

Several members of the Aikau family were gathered together on the grass, and there was a distinctive, collective hoot as he pulled into his tube ride.

Two of the Pipeline guys, Burns and Derek Ho, were surfing beautifully backside. Up on the beach, public-address announcer Lord "Tally Ho" Blears was reminiscing about Eddie.

"I remember those distinctive shorts of his, I think they were black and yellow," he said.

"Red and white!" someone from the Aikau family yelled back, angrily. Tally Ho, a dear man and an institution at Hawaiian surf meets, didn't have his best day at the mike.

Heat Six: Bradshaw was having a miserable day, from start to finish. He was having a miserable *winter*. In the weeks preceding the contest, he broke his three favorite boards for Waimea—"and in really stupid ways," he said. "Twice I was caught inside, the other time the board just buckled trying to get out at Sunset. The night before the contest, I was up sanding a couple of brand-new boards. Couldn't believe it. After four years, all that waiting, I wasn't ready. I was using equipment I'd never even ridden."

Bradshaw said he was "heartbroken" after the first heat, when he couldn't pull the trigger on either of the two big sets. "I didn't feel good at all," he said. "I didn't like anything that was happening. The life was gone. The enthusiasm was gone. It's like I wasn't even there."

On the first wave of his final heat, Bradshaw had a chance to gain some ground. It was a good-sized beast, and he had position. But in this contest, "position" didn't mean much. Surfers on the inside (riding the deepest) got an edge in points, but there was no penalty for dropping in. And if that inside rider got snuffed and you kept going, you came out the winner. "I mean, people were actually *encouraged* to drop in," said Bradshaw. "That was another mistake I made. I didn't know they were interpreting the rules that way."

At any rate, the Japanese surfer, Kuga, dropped in on Bradshaw. Actually, he free-fell in. Kuga mis-timed his entry and as Bradshaw was streaking down the wave, Kuga was falling from the sky. "A guy who shouldn't even be *in* the contest," Bradshaw said. "That completely threw me off, and the wave just blew me apart."

Typical of the day he was having, Bradshaw's leash came off his ankle and the board washed all the way to the beach. This was about the only impressive moment Bradshaw had, swimming in, grabbing his second new board, then getting back out in plenty of time for more waves. That didn't surprise Jack Shipley a bit.

"In one of the Sunset contests this year, 25-minute heats, I saw Bradshaw break his leash on the peak—not the inside reef, the outside—swim all the way in, paddle back out, and still catch three scoring waves," said Shipley. "If Doerner is one of the top 10 fittest guys on the North Shore, Bradshaw is among the top five."

But it was no consolation to Bradshaw. He finished 30th in the contest, with only Lynch, Rothman and Kealoha behind him. "Kenny fought the waves, instead of flowing with 'em," said Doerner. "He couldn't put anything together."

Nor could Foo, who finished a more respectable 14th but didn't catch the waves he wanted. "There were two heats with really pumping waves—Brock's heats—and I wasn't in them," said Foo. "I take losses pretty hard, but it's OK, now I'm just more motivated again. My mother likes going to psychics, consulting the stars, stuff like that, and she kept asking when I was going to win. She wants me to quit, you know. She kept getting the same answer: 1991. *Not* this year. So she said, 'Mark, I guess it means the gods want you to stay in the sport longer.' And it's true. I have a better perspective now. I don't care how long I have to wait."

Foo said he'd learned an interesting lesson from Downing, a couple of months before the contest. It was November 2, Darrick Doerner's day at Waimea, and the morning Foo had gone to Makaha. "I saw Keone paddle out for his first wave," Mark said. "And this guy doesn't surf a whole lot.

So it's a 15-foot wave, a perfect wall, and he just stood there, getting deeper and deeper. He back-doored the bowl, and just came out dry. I think that was the most amazing ride I've ever seen, especially at that size.

"Now, this guy's been surfing for 30 years, probably 20 at Makaha," said Foo. "It took him 30 years to catch that wave. It made me realize what longevity really means in this sport. Brock and I used to go out in anything. Onshore winds, 20 feet, nobody else out, but we'd call each other, 'cause we knew the other guy would go. And you'd end up hurting yourself, breaking your board, something. And just recently, on about an 18-20-foot stormy day, Brock and I just shined it.

"So I told Keone about us not going out, and he said, 'Ah, you're getting smart. And you know why? Because you know you're gonna surf big waves, anyway. You might as well just wait for the good days.' That made a lot of sense. I mean, Keone came over to Waimea that day and didn't even go out. He went back to Makaha and caught the wave of his life."

Downing, still in the flow, had another great heat. Good things just kept coming his way. But it was Schmidt who blew everyone away. There had been a long lull in this final hour, and I remember Owl Chapman saying, "It just stopped." But suddenly, an ominous-looking set was spotted from the dead north—a freak, on this day of west swells. A collective "Oh, shit" went up from the surfers who understood the consequence, because this set looked *mean*. "I have these really far-out-there binoculars, and I focused in on Schmidt," said Shipley. "He was paddling right for it. In 1974, Reno Abellira had a ride that won him the contest. This thing was a winning wave. Richard was 40 feet on the other side of the peak, just angling in, when he took off."

The 29-year-old Schmidt had been smoking-hot all winter, winning the Hawaiian pro contest at 15-foot Sunset and finishing third in the Triple Crown's Hard Rock event. "When I saw that set feathering on the horizon, I started talking myself into doing it," he said. "Usually I'm 100 percent positive, but this wave was at least 25 feet, and at that size, your survival instinct tells you to paddle over it. Maybe you don't want this. But with the contest on, and the crowd and all that, I figured I'd just go for it."

As soon as Schmidt got to his feet, the wave sucked out underneath him and he was pitched into the air. He dropped a good 10 feet through open space. "On a glassy day, my board would have just dropped away," he said. "But the wind kept it right underneath me. I felt like I was just floating—and then I landed."

In a spectacular display of balance and positive thinking, Schmidt was still in the wave. He got to the bottom, turned, and rode it out. "I was so ecstatic," he said. "That was probably the heaviest wave of my life. It was the epitome of big-wave riding—putting yourself at the most critical point, on the biggest wave, and coming out unscathed. I was just shaking with adrenalin."

The score: a perfect 100. "But I'm telling you, that was at least 10 points better than Brock's ride," said Shipley. "We cheated Richard. You can't score a performance like his. The system cannot allow for a ride that good."

It took nearly an hour for the judges to sort it all out. Finally the results came in: Doerner sixth, Clyde fifth, Michael Ho fourth, Schmidt third, Little second... and in a slice of pure *Hawaiiana*, Keone Downing first. Downing remembered driving home that night and thinking, "What an incredible day of surfing. I mean, for everybody. The whole event, the people on the beach, up on the cliff, down the road, the energy was so positive. The wind came out of the valley, which it never does, and everybody was hooting each other on in the water. The bigger the sets, the louder the hoots.

"I was completely focused," he said. "In my mind, when athletes talk about times when they really excel, it's because they're in tune that day. Nothing distracts them. That can be difficult in big waves, but I didn't let anything in—the elements, the games your mind wants to play. I didn't even *see* the

175

other people."

Later that night, Downing and Barton Lynch stopped to have dinner, and they encountered a Midwestern couple who had seen the event. "After a while, I mentioned we'd been in it," he said. "We talked for a long time, just commenting on how beautiful the whole thing was, before it ever came up how we'd done. I finally said I'd won it, but to them, it was the whole afternoon that mattered. That's what Eddie's surfing was all about. Not to be flamboyant, or to brag about how you can ride big waves. Just grab your board, do it, and go home. These days don't come that often, and when they do, it's a special thing just to participate. It was a magical day."

"Keone could do no wrong," Grigg would say later. "He was like Joe Montana: totally in control, and mentally dominating. We used to call George Downing the Desert Fox, because he was always the strategist, always in the right place. I saw that in Keone today."

"Keone does everything right, wherever he goes," said Doerner. "In his car, at the market, in business, in the water. He learned from the water. Today was his reward. The waves came to him."

As the sun went down off Kaena Point, each of the top three finishers addressed the crowd—briefly, humbly. "I thought I was diggin' my own grave," said Schmidt. Little, after a few words of thanks, held up a finger and said, "I just want to say that Darrick Doerner surfs out here really well. And thanks to Bradshaw and Erickson for helping me out."

Keone Downing simply said this: "I surfed in the memory of Eddie Aikau. And I dedicated my surfing to Pops."

Let it rest that way.

Big Wednesday

It took him nearly 30 years, but Ken Bradshaw finally understood what Greg Noll was talking about.

Back in '69, Noll walked away from surfing after catching an inconceivably large wave at Makaha. It was said to be 30 to 35 feet, Hawaiian style. At the time it was the biggest wave ever ridden—isolate it from tow-in surfing, and it still might have that distinction—and Noll barely survived the moment. Sitting farther outside than the other dozen brave souls in the water that day, Noll stroked into the beast, successfully made the drop, then watched a mountain of water about to descend upon him. He calmly jumped off his board, felt a second of two of utter peace, then got swirled, pounded and punished for what seemed like an eternity.

Safely on the beach, Noll pondered his life in the ocean. He was in his 30s now, no longer the young gun of Hawaiian big-wave surfing. He'd ridden everything from 18-foot Sunset to second-reef Pipeline to 25-foot Waimea Bay. He was The Bull, the man among men, the standard by which others were judged. And now came this seminal moment, almost surreal as it measured so much higher than his other accomplishments. He had just ridden the biggest wave. And he flat-out retired— realizing, as he has often said, "There wasn't a hell of a lot more I could do."

If Bradshaw had a difficult time fathoming Noll's decision, he wasn't alone. How can anyone walk away from surfing, at any age? It's a sport for a lifetime, fit for little kids, grown women, mature men and low-key cruisers in their 50s, 60s and 70s. No thing in the world can replace the satisfaction of leaving the water after a good session; the feeling never goes away. Bail out on Hawaii, that's one thing ... but abandon the sport altogether?

"As much as I knew about Greg, and his passion for surfing, the whole thing just seemed strange to me," said Bradshaw.

Then came the Wednesday morning of January 28, 1998, the high point of a raging El Niño winter. Waves up to 40 feet were reported in Hawaii during a swell so massive, the Eddie Aikau contest was called off without the slightest hesitation. It was the ultimate Big Wednesday, and nobody wanted any part of Waimea Bay. But Bradshaw, along with a half-dozen other tow-in crews, had other ideas. He and his partner, Dan Moore, ventured to Outside Log Cabins, the ultimate Oahu location for outer-reef perfection. Out there, Bradshaw was towed into the largest wave ever ridden on the North Shore. Nobody even disputed the notion—it was just that apparent. Bradshaw's wave was in the mythical 40-foot realm, a cut above most of the waves ridden that day (including the shot of Bradshaw on the cover of this book), and he didn't just survive it. He carved a huge bottom turn and pulled up into the hook before easing onto the shoulder, where Moore picked him up on the jet-ski.

Bradshaw had an unbelievable session that day. He caught two other waves in the 35-foot range and maybe 20 others at around 25 feet, pretty much the minimum size for this mythical break between Waimea and Pipeline. For a few hours, he soaked up the euphoria of the moment, got high-fived by every serious surfer in sight, and savored the realization of exactly what he'd done.

And then he fell into depression. Back out at Sunset, his favorite spot, Bradshaw found nothing but frustration in the coming days. The waves were perfect and a solid 12 feet, but he couldn't recapture that feeling. He couldn't find the speed, the raw power of his turns, anything even approaching the magnitude of that outer-reef session. He began to realize that at the age of 45, he may have only ten years left in his big-wave prime—and that a swell like January 28 might not come around for a quarter-century.

"He's a little nuts to be around right now," said Layne Beachley, Bradshaw's loving companion and the best big-wave rider in the world of women's surfing. "He's just not doing very well."

As Bradshaw described it, "It's kind of like a post-orgasmic depression. Even when Waimea broke a couple of days later, I couldn't get into it. Being at Outside Logs was something I'd dreamed about, planned for, thought about for almost 20 years. All of a sudden it happened. And then it was gone. It was such a high, so fulfilling, life after that was just anticlimactic. I was like, wow ... now what? For the first time, I got a handle on that Greg Noll thing."

About a month later, Bradshaw rediscovered the old stoke. It took something dramatic to restore his motivation, and it wasn't the North Shore, where the month of March unfolded with mostly medium-range surf. It was the notion of towing in at Jaws, at Maverick's, any new frontier he could find.

"There are so many places out there," he said. "I've never been out at Jaws, but I think those guys are ready for me to come over. There are other places in Hawaii that I want to go experience. I started thinking about Maverick's and that whole north coastal area, just a bumper land waiting to be discovered. That started motivating me. It was great. I got over that emotional depression and got back to living life again."

Bradshaw might have been depressed in the wake of his Outside Logs session, but he was the toast of surfing. They swarmed all over him at the trade show in Southern California. Every big-wave local on the North Shore either witnessed his ride in person, from roofs or hillsides, or saw it on video. "I've had guys telling me what an inspiration I am," said Bradshaw.

"They're all, 'Are you really 45 years old? Cause if you are, man, I'm 27, and if I take care of myself, I'll still be in my prime 20 years from now.' That's very gratifying."

I had the good fortune of being on the North Shore that memorable January 28. I had arrived the night before to stay at the home of longtime Pipeline lifeguard Mark Cunningham and his wife, Linny, and as we drove to dinner that night, we stopped by George Downing's surf shop, just to hear what Downing had to say about the rumored swell. As usual, he was skeptical. The buoys were relatively dead. "A lot of these things have potential," said Downing, who makes the "go" call on the Eddie Aikau contest. "But how many of them really come through?"

We were at Cunningham's house near midnight when a call came in from George Mason, the veteran Hawaii surf forecaster. He was breathless. I've never heard him so excited. "It's just now hitting, this is the one," he said. "It's gonna be 35 feet with great conditions." So it was no problem getting up before daybreak. After hearing that, it was difficult getting to sleep.

We were parked at Waimea Bay when the first light graced the North Shore. Even in the still and gentle warmth of a perfect morning, the place was unrecognizable. You couldn't even find the break. At times it looked like an enormous left, throwing death waves into the corner. Then the middle of the Bay would close out. Then some hideous set would loom far to the north, peeling in the distance, looking like it might have some potential until it hit the inside reef, sucked dry and threw— totally unrideable and looking to be some 60 feet on the faces.

The beach was filled with big-wave surfing legends, none of them making a move for their boardshorts, wax or bravado. They just stood there and watched. Days later, some of them said they would have been ready. Randy Rarick wasn't sure. "I asked everyone of 'em that morning," said Rarick, who was helping Downing organize the event. "Nobody wanted to go out there."

Jay Moriarity, who had a spot on the alternates' list, said, "I was just in awe. I'd never seen anything like that before. The whole ocean came alive and put on a show. You guys ain't going surfing today. You're just going to watch."

Bradshaw couldn't believe the Aikau was even a possibility. "You'll notice nobody's out," he said. "You can't *get* out."

"It wouldn't be a contest," said lifeguard Mark Dombrowski. "It would be people running for their lives."

"Outside Logs is the call," said Brock Little. "Biggest and best rideable waves in the world. Bigger than Jaws. It's gonna be unreal."

Everyone was stealing glances at Brock, the man generally expected to charge the hardest at big Waimea. "It was crazy to even consider it," he said a few days later. "If they had told me to go, I would have paddled out there, probably to my doom. I'll do it. I'm kind of cocky in that manner. If someone else is going to paddle out, then I'll paddle out. I don't give a shit."

As the waiting-for-Eddie morning progressed, it became evident that several notable figures were missing. Darrick Doerner was in California, reportedly attending to some family-related business. Tom Carroll and Jeff Clark couldn't catch the flights they needed to arrive in time. Kelly Slater, having already pulled the trigger on one Aikau alert, decided to stay in Florida. Bodyboarder Mike Stewart was stuck in California on business and also took a pass.

Stewart's absence had a direct effect on Little, because the two are tow-in partners. With his mind on Outside Log Cabins, Brock appeared to be in eminently good hands as he arrived at Haleiwa Harbor—the only remotely safe place to attempt a launch—with Ocean Safety mainstays Brian Keaulana, Terry Ahue and Mel Pu'u. But this swell had everyone freaked out. A state-mandated order forced closure of the harbor, and even Keaulana, considered to be Hawaii's top all-around waterman, wasn't allowed to go out there.

"I had to respect Brian and Terry, because they were dealing with their bosses," said Brock. "If it had been just me and Mike ... fuck it, we would have gone out there, anyway."

Stewart confirmed that, saying, "Throw me in jail later, but I'm out there. I would have launched at frickin' Leftovers, if I had to (the Leftovers-Alligators area is where Todd Chesser died last winter). But I'm out there. Brock and I have been waiting five years for this. Missing that day . . . I'm just sick. I feel like I'm mourning the death of a friend."

Brock was beside himself. Deep down, he wanted to drag Keaulana's crew up to Sunset for a tow-in launch. But the traffic was insane; it seemed that everyone on Oahu had turned out to watch the surf. Putting his personal interests aside, and knowing that Keaulana was leaning heavily toward Makaha, Brock jumped in a truck and headed for the West Side.

Part of me wanted to stay on the North Shore, find a good spot in the hills, and watch whatever tow-in action might take place. But Cunningham was intent on joining the Little-Keaulana tow-in session, just to add his presence as a safety measure. And Cunningham had the car. Figuring Makaha might be all-time, I jumped in for the ride.

About an hour later, Brock's three-ski crew hit the water at the Waianae lifeguard substation. The group included Keaulana, Ahue, Pu'u, lifeguards Cunningham, Mike Hart and Kawika Foster, and Ronald Hill, a relatively unknown big-wave surfer from the Little-Chesser-Ross Williams generation. I took the wheel of Cunningham's rig and embarked on a most promising journey: Tooling around the West Side on one of the biggest, cleanest days of the last 25 years.

Makaha didn't serve up the 20-foot point surf some were expecting, but it was a pristine 12-to-15 feet, loaded with world-class surfers and challenging as hell. "I just got caught inside a 15-foot set," said 60-year-old Ricky Grigg, totally stoked, his eyes sparkling. "It was just so beautiful, looking at this big green wall coming down. Broke my leash. But I'm goin' back out for more."

Nostalgia was playing a major part that day. Rarick, who is pushing 50, had a soul-stirring session on a 10-0 balsa board that he shaped himself. "I've pretty much given up surfing big Waimea," he said. "I feel like I've reached my peak. But it was incredible out there. I felt absolutely as strong as ever. Totally confident."

Rarick had met up with a Santa Cruz contingent—Moriarity, Jim Richards and Richard Schmidt—for the occasion. "It was the first time I'd surfed it with that much size," said Moriarity. "What an awesome wave ... breaking from out at the point all the way across. The end bowl can get you pretty good, because it stands up and you have to stay super high and race through it. If you don't it will clip you. There were maybe 20 guys out and everyone was in a good mood. I got some good ones but ended up breaking my 10-0. We all got caught and five of us had broken boards."

That was my last vision at Makaha, the sight of a smiling Moriarity walking up and down the beach, politely asking if anyone had a 10-0. I figured Brock and the boys had headed up to Kaena Point, and I was hoping to catch at least a glimpse through my binoculars. As it turned out, they stopped short of Kaena and had a tremendous tow-in session at outside Makua Cave, a spot that to Keaulana's knowledge had never been ridden. But I'll never forget what I saw at Kaena: Indescribably beautiful 40-foot waves, monstrous and peeling, blue-green against the late-afternoon light. Even from a mile's distance, they came majestically to life. Forget anything you've seen at Jaws or anywhere else; if challenged, these would have been the biggest waves ever attempted.

"I think if it had been just Brock, Brian and Mel, they would have gone out there," said Cunningham. "But we had a lot of baggage, myself included. Not everyone in that crew was ready for waves that big. We made the safe call at Makua, and those guys just went off."

Not that Brock enjoyed it much. Back on land, he was still stewing about leaving the North Shore—and he hadn't even heard the news yet. He didn't hear what went down with Bradshaw, Noah Johnson, Aaron Lambert and the rest of the dozen-odd surfers who experienced Outside Log Cabins.

"Don't even tell me about it," said Brock. "I know all about Outside Logs. I see it every day when I drive from Pupukea Road, and I've been fantasizing about the place since 1983. I've seen it even bigger than Wednesday. I've seen it 10 feet bigger and I know for a fact that it will never close out. I'm just bitter about the whole thing."

These were the tow-in crews who motored into history that day:

• Ross Clarke-Jones and Tony Ray, two Australians who charge every big wave they can find in Hawaii or anywhere else.

• Cheyne Horan, another Australian who has grown comfortable in gigantic Hawaiian surf, and Sam Hawk, a North Shore legend from the 1970s who has retreated comfortably into the background in recent years.

• Michael and Milton Willis, the wave-stoked brothers who live right at Sunset Point and devote their lives to big surf.

• Shawn Briley, hellman extraordinaire, and Kawika Standt, one of the North Shore's underground mainstays.

• North Shore locals Noah Johnson, Aaron Lambert and Troy Alotis, alternating drivers and riders in a three-way assault.

• Bradshaw and Dan Moore, about to rack up the most mind-blowing tow-in session ever enjoyed on the island of Oahu.

Surfers have been watching and reading about Bradshaw since the early '70s, when he moved to Hawaii from Encinitas (by way of his native Texas). But who the heck is Dan Moore? Who's the guy Bradshaw trusts above all in life-threatening conditions? Who forms the second half of this team, unquestionably the most dedicated, experienced and professional on the North Shore?

He's a 41-year-old contractor who grew up in Melbourne Beach, Fla., and bailed to Hawaii—for good—at the age of 17. Moore was a competitive surfer for a while but never took to the scene, "and I never did that well in contests," he said. "I was more into my career, trying to get ahead with my contracting work.

"I first met Ken in 1976, at the Pro Class Trials competition at Haleiwa. He was in one of my heats. But we didn't start hanging out and surfing together until the late '80s, out of necessity, because we both wanted to surf the outer reefs and it was hard to find someone else to go out there. It was always, like, "Nobody else is going out, I better call Bradshaw ... he'll go (laughter)."

Moore is a highly competent strapped-in surfer and, like Bradshaw, a top-notch driver. Asked if he had any regrets about his underground status, he said, "I suppose if I'd wanted it, I could have made some sort of name for myself, but I didn't put the time and energy into promoting myself. It wasn't a priority. I don't thrive on it. I'm just out there because I love to do it. Not to make money or anything else. I'm still a full-time contractor ... unless it's macking. Then I don't go to work (laughs)."

This marked the third straight winter that Bradshaw and Moore were tow-in partners, and their experience really paid off. "Phantoms was the only place to launch that day, and it was sketchy at best," said Moore. "I've never seen it closing out like it was, from Revelations all the way through to Kammieland. There was no getting around it. You were gonna have to jump waves—it was just a matter of where and how many. Ken and I must have sailed 12 feet in the air going over one. The whole thing was just unbelievable. But we weren't the least bit anxious or nervous about the situation. All the elements came together, and we were mentally prepared for it."

As for his own surf session, Moore said, "I took one doughnut. I did a faceplant down in the pit, probably a 25-footer, and it gave me a good spanking. Then I went back over the falls and it spanked me again. But it was a great session considering how many waves we got ... I'd say 25 or 30 apiece. On the way back to shore, Ken and I couldn't stop congratulating each other. We knew how much we killed it. It was a pretty touching moment."

Like Bradshaw, Moore felt that odd rush of withdrawal in the aftermath. "Trying to paddle into some waves at Sunset the next day was really frustrating," he said. "Most of the time, I feel like a kook trying to get back on a regular board. You have to physically force yourself to get back to that level ... not to mention the crowd factor. I'm telling you, this (tow-in surfing) has changed a lot of lives. Certainly ours. I'm possessed now."

Another North Shore contractor, veteran big-wave rider Bill Sickler, watched his old friend Bradshaw from the hills above Pupukea that day. He was completely blown away.

"Ken got a stand-up barrel that was approaching 35 feet," said Sickler. "Had to be the most beautiful wave I've ever seen. Glassy and peeling, like Backdoor blown out of proportion. Ken was surfing beautifully. The gods were smiling on him. He couldn't do anything wrong."

As Bradshaw recalled it, "Dan and I surfed three hours, had lunch, then went back for a two-hour session. It was a little bumpy in the morning, but it was so big and hollow, it was OK. The afternoon session was velvet. Totally still, mind-blowing massive. I felt like I was slicing through butter on my 7-10 at 45 miles an hour. My biggest wave was in the morning, but I got another 30-plus wave in the afternoon. Aaron Lambert came up to me and said, 'As long as I live, I'll have that view in my mind.' And Dan was like, 'That's it! That was fuckin' beyond cartoon!' He was like a little kid."

Some other observations on the day (thanks to Ben Marcus for his interview contributions):

Peter Mel: "I watched the whole session from the roof of Ethan Powell's house on Ke Iki Road. It was just an awesome thing to be a part of. Perfect conditions, slight offshore, just as nice as you could ever have it, and the biggest waves ever ridden. My call is that Aaron Lambert got the best-ridden wave of the day. He did a big hook in the pit and then he did another one. But everybody was going off. If anyone tells you the stories of that day are an exaggeration, they're wrong."

Cheyne Horan: "I was riding a 7'7 with straps, built by Geoff McCoy. It's a heavy board, 17 inches wide. I had some exciting moments, but the best was going up to the top and snapping back as the lip was coming over on a 30-foot wave. Those were the biggest waves I've ever surfed in. If you saw someone coming off a huge bottom turn out there, it didn't even look real. It felt like the whole planet was breaking."

Ross Clarke-Jones: "I reckon the first wave I caught was 30 feet, and that's being modest. It was surreal out there. I got like four waves, and on the fourth one Tony put me in a little deep. We were going as fast as we could, and when I let go I was going faster than Tony, but neither of us were going fast enough. That ski just couldn't outrun the wave. It collected me and Tony and we both got smashed.

"I popped up screaming, where the fuck is Tony? I couldn't see him anywhere and then I saw this patch of purple floating around. It was the seat of the Jet Ski. I finally saw Tony a little farther out than me. Tony and the ski were getting dragged to shore with the ski full of water when Aaron Lambert came to the rescue. He towed Tony and the ski back outside into the channel.

"I was spewing. I was so pissed off that I lost my board and that we might lose the ski. Tony and I had spent almost 10 grand on the thing. Kawika Standt and Shawn Briley got there with a bigger ski and they towed us through Haleiwa Harbor. That was incredible in itself. The waves were closing out between Avalanche and Puaena Point and I was thinking, Oh my God, how are we going to get in? It was a mad ride but we made it.

"We managed to salvage the ski. We have the least expensive one, the Yamaha WaveRunner II. That's the standard lifeguard ski, but it wasn't enough for us that day. Not for what we were willing to do. Our ski is a 750 cc (Bradshaw and Moore have the 1100). I think we're going for a bigger one, because this one didn't cut it."

Noah Johnson: "This is such a new thing, we really don't know what we're doing. We haven't done it enough. This is only like the third time Aaron and I have done it together in any kind of size, and we're really unorganized. We just use the skis to get us on the waves and then ride them like normal. And if we fall in the pit, we're going to take a few waves on the head. We're not counting on the ski to pick us up afterward. We're just not. We haven't done it enough to be totally sure of doing that. We don't even have a sled on our ski right now. We're trying to head in the direction of the Maui guys, where we get rescues down.

"I pulled Troy (Alotis) into a crazy closeout, backside. I think I put a little warble on it with my wake, and I wish I hadn't done that. He would have had a much better chance. But I didn't think he was going to pull in. I was going, 'Whaaat?' It was heavy. The whole day ... it was probably the most amped I'd ever been in my life. We were jumping up and down, high-fiving each other on the ski. It was crazy.

"I guess the whole North Shore was watching, yeah. It was kind of weird thinking about that. It's been the buzz and the talk and everything. It was like the biggest playground you could ever have handed to you. Our faces were all cracking from smiling. I still can't believe it actually came together. I've just been running around in circles getting ready for the next one. But it's a bummer ... I'm starting to realize that it may not happen again in my lifetime."

Bill Sickler, the long-respected mainstay of big-wave riding on the North Shore, was watching through binoculars from his home in Pupukea Heights. He was up there with Peter Cole and Charlie Walker, and the three of them were completely blown away—could hardly believe what they were seeing.

"It was such a pleasure to watch Noah Johnson out there. I've never really seen him before," said Sickler. "I knew he charged, but I didn't know he did it with such assurance. He made it look like he'd been out there a hundred times before. He'd go over behind the peak of these waves, and the driver, too, and they'd start bombing parallel across, full blast, so deep it was unbelievable. I saw Noah disappear in the tube for about 3 to 4 seconds, in the top half of the wave, and come out of a wave well over 30 feet. Later he had to straighten out on one, and the thing just crushed him. He had to go underneath the next wave, easily the biggest wave I've ever seen someone go under. A 35-foot set, easy. There was so much whitewater frothing, I was beginning to wonder if he could get a breath if he *did* come up. And shit, he jumps back up on the tow handles and heads out for another one.

"This kid's gonna be unbelievable. Charlie (Walker) and I were just blown away. When he went out there, he just took command. He gave you this feeling it wasn't this haphazard bullshit. And Ross Clarke-Jones is just exceptional. He's like Brock, just the best there is. He caught the first one that I saw and my god, he cooked. He's peaking right now, he's right at that age. He's kind of like Bradshaw used to be … and obviously still is."

Sickler paused for a moment. "I can't believe I'm throwing out '30 feet' and '35 feet' like it's nothing. Most of us, guys who've ridden Waimea Bay for years, can count the number of 25-footers we've caught on one hand. It's just a whole new dimension out there."

Imagine a 45-year-old man catching the biggest wave ever ridden on Oahu. At that age, football players are telling old war stories and limping around on bad knees. Basketball players have lost their lift. Gymnasts and track stars are 20 years past their prime. Tennis and volleyball players are on low-cruise, still enjoying life but not blowing away the competition. Ken Bradshaw is 45 and at the absolute peak of the surfing world. What a glowing endorsement for the sport.

There are no photos of Bradshaw's ultimate wave on Big Wednesday, the bomb he caught that morning. Not a single snapshot. And here's why: Bradshaw didn't alert the media that day. He didn't call the magazines, collar some personal photographer or announce his intentions to the world. He just went surfing. Just as he's done for 25 years. That's so

189

perfect, too. Unless you're Kelly Slater, Laird Hamilton or Lisa Andersen, that's the story of all our lives. Have you ever had your best wave filmed, or captured on video? Did you ever wish that just once, you'd have a killer photo of a lifetime wave? Bradshaw wouldn't mind having one, but he's not that worried about it. He's got the image in his mind. And that's all he needs.

The Last Wave

On the 23rd of December, 1994, Mark Foo died at Maverick's. It was his first trip to the famed big-wave break in Northern California, and he perished on what was, for him, a relatively harmless wave. This was the author's account in the San Francisco Chronicle.

The hardy surfers of Northern California spent long evenings of soul-searching over the holiday weekend, trying to sort out Mark Foo's death. They all knew someone would be killed at Maverick's someday. They could even accept it happening to one of the sport's most heroic figures.

But there was an unsettling aspect to that afternoon in Half Moon Bay, something strange and incomprehensible. Foo's body floated for nearly an hour, unnoticed, before it was discovered on a breakwater near the harbor entrance—some three-quarters of a mile from the spot of the accident.

The place had never been more crowded. On a normal surfing day—maybe a dozen times a year—Maverick's is a stark, remote outpost on the coastline, populated by just a handful of surfers, photographers and onlookers. But this day had the feel of a Super Bowl, a major event. Word had spread quickly that Foo, Brock Little and Ken Bradshaw would be flying in from Hawaii, representing the elite of big-wave surfing, and nobody wanted to miss out.

There were three boats in the water, each filled with photographers. Some 150 people lined the cliffs. A helicopter

191

buzzed overhead, manned by Surfer Magazine staffers. The lineup of surfers represented some of the bravest and most safety-conscious in the sport. It seemed the entire surfing establishment had descended upon Maverick's that day.

And yet, nobody saw Mark Foo. It's quite possible that he died within moments after being struck in the head by his board, that he drowned in the raging whitewater after being knocked unconscious. But nobody knows for sure, and for Dr. Mark Renneker, who joined Foo and a dozen others in the water that day, the notion is difficult to shake.

"I've been trying to find some perspective on this," said Renneker, 42-year-old founder of the Surfers Medical Association and one of the most respected big-wave surfers in the world. "Was it a natural or unnatural death? It isn't merely the euphemism of, well, he died doing what he loved to do. Because to me, it was an act of violence, a violent act of nature. I liken it to a mugging in the middle of Times Square on New Year's Eve, where you expect hundreds of people to have witnessed it and somehow done something about it. And yet, the event went completely unnoticed. He just disappeared."

The distinguished array of surfers included Mike Parsons, considered the best at Todos Santos, the noted big-wave spot in Mexico; Evan Slater, fast becoming known as the hottest surfer on the Ocean Beach-Maverick's circuit; San Francisco regulars John Raymond, Steve Lowry and Bill (Pee Wee) Bergeson, and Santa Cruz standouts Peter Mel, Josh Loya and Jay Moriarity. Didn't any of them realize the severity of Foo's wipeout?

"Normally we work on the buddy system out there," said Renneker. "Any time somebody takes off, everybody else watches to see what happens. But on this particular day, a sort of mass intoxication was in effect. It wasn't a big day for Maverick's—maybe 15 to 18 feet, compared to 20 feet-plus earlier in the week. It was incredibly pleasant—beautiful, calm weather when it's usually ice-cold and windy. The surf media seemed to have it fully documented. There was almost a sense that nothing could go wrong. And Mark was the kind of confident, self-contained person who is successful in everything he does."

When Foo failed to return to the lineup, the surfers figured he'd gone in to get a new board. The photographers focused immediately on the ensuing waves; that's their job. The midday glare and Maverick's vast playing field made it difficult for cliffside spectators to see anything in much detail. Up in the helicopter, said Surfer Magazine writer Matt Warshaw, "Foo's wipeout looked so unremarkable that we didn't even notice it. I'm ashamed to say that, but like everyone else, we were focused on the waves, particularly the one right after Mark's, when two of the biggest names in surfing were fighting for their lives."

On that wave, Little and Parsons took off together. Both wiped out, and with a westerly swell combining with northerly currents, both were swept into an area of large, unforgiving rocks, a horrible sort of no-man's land that nearly took the life of legendary Maverick's surfer Jeff Clark two winters ago. "Both of those guys had their boards stuck on the rocks, and they were hanging by their leashes, getting pounded by waves, unable to pull themselves up," said Renneker. "Brock told me later he thought it might be over. Parsons said he was talking to his parents, making amends with God. I mean, both of these guys were pale when I saw them later. Mark Foo was underwater, dead or dying, but people were focused on the visible, which was two of the finest big-wave riders in the world being dashed on the rocks."

As Warshaw looks back, "The ghastliest detail is that Parsons might have bumped into Foo's body at some point. He said he felt something underwater when he was getting thrashed around, and he figured it had to be Brock. Except that Brock was several yards away and said he didn't feel anything."

There was no search party for Foo. He was discovered only when a boatload of photographers and surfers, including Parsons, headed back to shore. "Foo had been floating face-down for probably an hour," said photographer Steve Spaulding. "We were coming into the harbor entrance when Evan Slater spotted something—it was the tailblock of Foo's board (broken in three pieces), still leashed to his leg."

Slater and Parsons both dove into the water, pulled on the leash and recoiled in horror. Frantic attempts at resuscitation were futile; Mark Foo was long gone.

The annals of surfing lore are filled with tragedy. Eddie Aikau died in the open ocean, trying to save the lives of people stranded on a capsized craft. Jose Angel went free-diving for black coral and never returned. Back in the '40s, Dickie Cross was battered to death by waves in the growing darkness at 30-foot Waimea Bay. Bob Simmons, already crippled by a gimpy arm, died surfing in La Jolla in the 1950s. But in terms of a world-class surfer being killed by a wave, there was no precedent for the significance of Foo's passing (the death of Todd Chesser, on Oahu's outer reefs near Leftovers, occurred two years later).

I knew Mark Foo fairly well. I spoke with him regularly during trips to the North Shore, and the news of his death shook my soul. Nobody was in better shape than Foo, nobody lived his life with more dedication to big-wave surfing. He often talked of surfing Waimea, Todos Santos and Maverick's on just the right swell in a three-day period. He lived in an elegant home where he could walk onto an upstairs perch and see the waves at Waimea. He was a surfing conglomerate unto himself—rider, author, television commentator, traveler—and he lived in abstinence of drugs, cigarettes and alcohol.

He was also a loner, a party of one. "I don't have any real friends," he told me once, and he seemed OK with that. He had given up everything, including a relationship with his parents, to pursue a single-minded assault on big waves. "Surfing is not what good Chinese boys do," said his sister, SharLyn Foo-Wagner. "They go to school, become doctors and lawyers. But Mark was at peace with himself. Many times he told me he was going to die young, and this (surfing) is how he wanted to go. Many times I heard him say, 'If you want to surf big waves, you have to be willing to pay the ultimate price.'"

He came to Maverick's because he couldn't stay away any longer. December 23 was the 11th day of an epic run of Northern California surf, unrivaled in the last 20 years for consistently massive waves and perfect conditions. Surfers had become nearly delirious with the scene, thrilled and exhausted and coming back for more, realizing it was a special time in their lives. It all peaked that Friday, a day from the textbook of surfing paradise. Not long after Mark Foo's body was found, the sweet easterly winds turned south. The sun gave way to fog and clouds. It was all over, and that night it rained without mercy.